Birnbaum's

Walt Disney World FOR KIDS BY KIDS

Jill Safro
Editor

Suzy Goytizolo
Senior Editor

Keith Groshans
Associate Art Director

Andrea Rotondo Hospidor
Contributing Editor

Linda Calderon
Editorial Assistant

Alexandra Mayes Birnbaum
Consulting Editor

THE OFFICIAL GUIDE

DISNEY EDITIONS AND HEARST BUSINESS PUBLISHING, INC.

ISBN: 0-7868-5315-8
Printed in the United States of America

An enormous debt of gratitude is owed to Kevin Banks, Darren Chiappetta, Laura Simpson, Darlene Papalini, Ken Potrock, Alain Boniec, Gene Duncan, Tim Lewis, Carolyn Ford Brunetto, Cathy Smith, Lynn Goytizolo, Mark Zaino, Noelle Vercesi, Kimberly Babb, Arlene Cullen, Donna Pascarella, and Beverly Schlitt, all of whom performed above and beyond the call of duty to make the creation of this book possible. To Phil Lengyel, Tom Elrod, Linda Warren, Bob Miller, and Charlie Ridgway, thank you for believing in this project in the first place. And to Wendy Lefkon, special thanks for taking it from idea to reality.

We'd also like to tip our hats to Tom Passavant, editorial director, and to Robert Rohr, copy editor extraordinaire.

Other 2001 Birnbaum's Official Disney Guides

Disneyland
Walt Disney World
Walt Disney World Without Kids

CONTENTS

You're Going to Disney World!

When you first heard the news, you couldn't believe your own ears. Could it be true? Were you really going on a vacation to Walt Disney World? Well, believe it or not, it's true! Before you know it, you'll be in the sunny state of Florida. It's the home of Walt Disney World and the most famous mouse on planet Earth. (Hint: His name starts with "M.")

If you have ever been there, you already know that it's one mighty big place with lots to do. In fact, there is so much going on that it can get a little confusing. That's where this book comes in handy. It describes everything in the World, from the Magic Kingdom theme park to the Hoop-Dee-Doo Musical Revue. And it's filled with advice from kids like you.

There is no right or wrong way to read this book. You can start on the first page and read straight through to the end. Or you can skip around, read your favorite parts first, and come back to the rest later.

No matter what you do, one thing is for sure: When you're done, you will be a true-blue Disney expert. Soon kids may start asking *you* for advice on how to have the most awesome vacation in the World!

Pack a Pencil and
Take Me Along With You!

Don't leave this book behind when you head for the parks. It's full of tips and opinions that you'll want to remember. There are games and activities, too. So don't forget to bring a pen or pencil. Here are some ways to use this book while visiting the wonderful world of Disney:

Track Your Trip

Each time you check out an attraction, check it off in this book. Then you'll know what's left to see on your next visit.

Play Detective

Sometimes waiting in line for a ride can seem to take forever. To make the time go faster, try to spot all of the objects hidden in Birnbaum's **line games** scavenger hunt. Every time you see Mickey on the lookout, there will be a clue to lead you on your way. Happy hunting!

Search for Hidden Mickeys

Disney Imagineers have hidden images of Mickey all over Walt Disney World. (Many look like the three connected circles that form Mickey's head.) You might see them in shadows, lights, drawings, or even in the clouds at some attractions. Look in this book for each Hidden Mickey Alert! to find a Hidden Mickey clue. Keep track of the number of Hidden Mickeys that you discover. That way when the trip is over you can write your findings on page 157 of this book's Magical Memories section.

Find the Fastpass

DISNEP'S
FASTPASS

How would you like to walk right up to the front of the line at some of the most popular rides? What? Cut the line? Yes, you sure can—if you have a Fastpass in your hand. You can get one for any ride that has a Fastpass symbol by its name in this book. They're free! Here's how it works: You get a ticket from the ride's Fastpass machine. It tells you when to come back. Then, return at that time, show a cast member your Fastpass ticket, and in just a few minutes you'll be on the ride!

We're Warning You!

Disney rides are full of surprises. That's part of what makes them so much fun. But not everyone likes surprises. So if things like loud noises or fast turns scare you, look at the book's **attraction reaction** warnings before you go on each ride. That way the only surprises you come across will be good ones!

The last four pages of this book are for autographs. Ask Disney characters to sign them!

5

Meet the Experts 2001

It's a lot of fun to work on a book like *Walt Disney World For Kids, By Kids*. But it's also a lot of hard work. Every year, a group of kids goes to Walt Disney World with the editors of *Birnbaum's Walt Disney World*. They spend days riding attractions, splashing in pools, and chomping on delicious munchies. (That's the fun part.) After each attraction the kids take notes about their experience in their Disney journals. (That's the work part.) They write about everything they did and saw. What's cool? What's not? Who chickened out at Space Mountain? The kids also try out all of the new activities and games. This book could not have been written without them.

Adam, Leah, Nicholas, and Jennifer (from left to right) had a blast working on this book!

Adam Pascarella lives in Frankfort, Illinois. He was 11 years old when he worked on this book. Adam enjoys spending time on the computer and has his own website. He also likes to play sports and the saxophone. His favorite Disney ride is Rock 'n' Roller Coaster.

Adam

Leah Cullen lives in Pittsburgh, Pennsylvania. She was 10 years old when she worked on this book. Leah is a vegetarian. She likes to play softball, ride her bike, and go rollerblading. Some day she wants to be a writer or a teacher. Her favorite Disney ride is Tower of Terror.

Leah

Nicholas Babb lives in Vancouver, Washington. He was 10 years old when he worked on this book. Nick is a boy scout and he loves to play soccer and basketball. His dream is to be an oceanographer. His favorite Disney ride is Tower of Terror.

Nicholas

Jennifer

Jennifer Schlitt lives in San Diego, California. She was 12 years old when she worked on this book. Jennifer loves to go swimming and play soccer. She also enjoys singing in her church choir. Her favorite Disney ride is Tower of Terror.

Eric L., David G., Grace H., and Jennifer B.

2000

1999

Kirsti H., Amy N., Seth R., and Robbie P.

1998

Danielle T., Dan M., Michael H., and Szasha O.

Brian F., Emma P., Adam F., and Ashley J.

1997

1994-1996

Adam W., Anna K., Danielle G., Dawna B., Bradley S., Tate L., Lindsay C., and Justin B.

Bonita B., Brain L., Robert R., Karyn W., Taran S., Ashley P., David B., and Elisabeth W.

Meet the Readers

Who can't get enough of Walt Disney World and has been there an average of four times? Our readers have! How do we know? You told us so. Every kid who wrote to us last year received a survey form to fill out. Those surveys helped us learn all about readers' interests and backgrounds.

What did we learn? For starters, a whole lot of you enjoy reading, drawing, writing, playing sports, and surfing the Web. Your favorite place to stay at WDW is the Caribbean Beach resort. You're starting to get a little tired of It's a Small World. But thrill rides like Tower of Terror are at the top of your list. And when you can't find a Mickey Mouse Ice Cream Bar to snack on, you love to chomp on a smoked turkey leg. Yum!

To everyone who filled out a survey, THANK YOU! We kept everyone's opinions in mind while we worked on this book.

Mickey is Number One!

It's probably not a surprise to hear that Mickey Mouse is the most popular Disney character with readers. But who would've guessed that Goofy would be a close second? Rounding out the top five faves are Winnie the Pooh, Tigger, and Pluto. Who's your favorite? Let us know!

Look for this Reader Pleaser ribbon throughout the book. We've placed it beside our readers' favorite Disney attractions, theme parks, snacks, and more. If you'd like to vote on next year's Reader Pleasers, write us a letter and we'll send you a survey form. Our address is listed below.

READER #1 PLEASER

READER TIP

Keep an eye out for this symbol. Every time you spot it, you'll find a great tip sent in by a reader. Do you have any Walt Disney World tips? We would love to hear them!

These are the big kids who had a great time helping to put this book together (from left to right: Keith, Suzy, and Jill).

PHOTO BY LINDA CALDERON

What do YOU think?

Do you agree or disagree with any of the kids in this book? Tell us! Send us a letter about your trip and a self-addressed stamped envelope to:

Birnbaum's Official Disney Guides
Kid Expert Applications
1790 Broadway, 6th Floor
New York, NY 10019

We will send you an application, and read every letter before we write next year's book.

Meet Walt Disney

Walt Disney was born in Illinois on December 5, 1901—that was one hundred years ago! During his life and in all the years since, Walt Disney's company created famous cartoons, movies, and theme parks, (and much, much more!) for everyone to enjoy. But how did it all begin?

Walt thought of Mickey as his own son.

Well, when Walt was a little boy he would look up at the sky and imagine the clouds were animals. As the wind pushed a cloud along, a pig would turn into a cow. Soon, the cow would become a chicken! It was then Walt realized that anything could become a reality with a little imagination.

But he knew that success wouldn't come from daydreaming alone. Growing up on a farm had taught him the importance of hard work. And it's a good thing, because without Walt's hard work we would never have met the most famous mouse in the world.

A mouse is born

Steamboat Willie was the first talking cartoon ever made.

In 1928, Walt created a little cartoon mouse—who he almost named Mortimer Mouse. Luckily, Lillian Disney convinced her husband to name him Mickey Mouse! Mickey's first movie was a black and white cartoon called *Steamboat Willie*. He was an instant success. But one hit wasn't enough for his creator. Walt was always looking for new challenges. In 1937, his animation company made the first full-length cartoon movie: *Snow White and the Seven Dwarfs*. Walt was very proud that he had made a movie for everyone in the family to enjoy.

Mickey's looks have changed a little bit over the years.

Family was very important to Walt. Every Sunday, he would do something special with his two daughters. He often took them to amusement parks. The kids loved it, but Walt was sad that there weren't rides for parents. "I wish there was a place where children *and* grown-ups could have fun," he thought.

A dream is a wish your heart makes

Since a place like that didn't exist, Walt decided to build it. At first he was going to call it Mickey Mouse Park, but then he named it Disneyland. Disneyland opened in Anaheim, California, in 1955. Families traveled from all over the world to visit it. Disneyland was so popular that Walt's new dream was to build an even bigger park: Disney World. He must have wished upon a star—because his dream came true.

Kids have loved Disneyland ever since it opened in 1955.

What a Wonderful World

Walt Disney loved dreaming up stories to tell and new ways to tell them. After he died, his brother, Roy, kept one of his biggest dreams alive. He made sure Walt's special "world" was built just the way Walt had imagined it. Roy even insisted that it be called *Walt* Disney World, so everyone would know it had been his brother's dream.

Walt Disney World officially opened on October 1, 1971. Since then, millions of people have stopped in for a visit. Some people come to Walt Disney World for a day, but most stay a little longer. There's just so much to see and do.

Pick a theme park, any theme park

The most famous part of Walt Disney World is the **Magic Kingdom**. It's home to Cinderella Castle, Space Mountain, and those rascally Pirates of the Caribbean. It's also where Mickey, Minnie, and their pals keep their country cottages. Kids of all ages can't get enough of this happy place. Of course, there are three other theme parks to see.

Epcot is a wonderland of science and discovery. Here you can take a Journey Into Your Imagination. It's also a great place to go on a "world tour." Lots of different countries have shops, restaurants, and attractions inside the theme park. Epcot opened in 1982.

Are you a major movie fan? If so, you'll get a big kick out of the **Disney-MGM Studios** theme park. It's jam-packed with movie-themed rides and exhibits. The secrets of animation are revealed at The Magic of Disney Animation. Belle and Gaston sing their hearts out at Beauty and the Beast Live on Stage. And The Twilight Zone Tower of Terror scares *everybody* silly. The Disney-MGM Studios opened in 1989.

Disney's Animal Kingdom is the newest theme park at Walt Disney World. (It got off to a *roaring* start in 1998.) It has what it takes to make any kid's day: an African safari ride filled with wild animals, life-like dinosaurs, and a super slimy 3-D movie about bugs.

Chill out!

Need to cool off on a hot day? You can make a splash at a Disney water park. Between **River Country**, **Typhoon Lagoon**, and **Blizzard Beach**, it's almost impossible to stay dry. Each one has slippery slides, tube rides, and some very cool pools.

But wait—there's more! Walt Disney World also has boats, bikes, and even horses to ride. It has hundreds of restaurants, shops, and other places to explore. In fact, no matter how many times you visit, there's always something new to see. Will Walt Disney World ever be finished? Not as long as there is imagination left in the world. That's exactly how Walt would have wanted it.

Magical Milestones

Big things are always happening in Disney's world. Here are a few of the greatest moments:

1901 — Walt Disney is born on December 5, in Chicago, Illinois.

1928 — Walt creates Mickey Mouse. Mickey stars in his first movie, *Steamboat Willie*.

1937 — Walt's animators finish *Snow White and the Seven Dwarfs*, the first full-length animated movie.

1955 — Walt's dream to make a family theme park comes true. Disneyland opens in Anaheim, California.

1971 — Walt Disney World (WDW) opens in Orlando, Florida.

1975 — Space Mountain, the first WDW roller coaster, opens.

1982 — Epcot opens at WDW.

1983 — Tokyo Disneyland opens in the capital city of Japan.

1987 — The first Disney Store has its grand opening in Glendale, California.

1989 — Disney-MGM Studios opens at WDW.

1992 — Disneyland Paris opens in France.

1996 — WDW celebrates its 25th anniversary.

1998 — Disney's Animal Kingdom opens at WDW.

2000 — Disney's Millennium Celebration takes over WDW.

2001 — The Magic Kingdom turns 30 years old. Wish it a happy birthday!

Getting Ready to Go

Planning a vacation to Walt Disney World is lots of fun. But it's not as easy as it sounds. There are so many choices to make! Which parks should you visit? What should you pack? And where can you meet your favorite Disney characters? Use this book to answer these questions and help plan your family's vacation. Remember: It's never too early to get started!

Make a Simple Schedule

Did you know that there are more than 300 attractions at Walt Disney World? It could take weeks to see them all. And most people don't have weeks to spend on vacation! That's why it's important to make a schedule before you leave home. Without it, you might miss some of the rides you want to try the most.

What You'll Need
● Paper ● Pencil ● This book

What to Do

1. Write "Magic Kingdom" on the top of a piece of paper.

2. Look at the Magic Kingdom chapter. Every time you see an attraction that sounds like fun, write its name on the paper.

3. When you have finished the chapter, look over your list. Then put a star next to your 10 favorite attractions. These are your "must-sees."

4. Now make a schedule for each of the other theme parks you plan to visit.

5. Don't forget to take your Simple Schedules to the parks!

Learn the Disney Lingo

Audio-Animatronics — Life-like robots, from birds and dinosaurs to movie stars and presidents. They seem real—but they're not.

Cast Member — A Disney employee.

Circle-Vision 360 — A movie that surrounds you. The screens form a circle.

Guidemap — A theme park map that also describes attractions, shops, restaurants, and entertainment.

Imagineer — A creative person who designs Disney attractions.

Save Room for Souvenirs

When you pack for your trip, make sure you're prepared for the weather. Believe it or not, it gets chilly in Florida, especially in the winter. But during the summer it's sizzling hot! It's usually warm during the rest of the year. Layers are a good idea, so you can take something off if you get hot. Remember to pack clothes and shoes that are lightweight and comfortable—since you'll do a lot of walking at the parks. And don't overstuff your suitcase. You'll need room for all the goodies you get at Walt Disney World.

What else should you bring? That's up to you! Here's a short list to help you get started:

- **A sweatshirt or sweater**
- **Broken-in sneakers or shoes**
- **Shorts and pants**
- **Long-sleeved and short-sleeved shirts**
- **A hat and sunglasses**
- **A bathing suit**
- **Sunscreen**

Visit Disney on the Internet

This book is chock-full of information about Disney, but there is another great place to learn about Walt Disney World: the Internet. Visit WDW's website at *www.disneyworld.com*.

If you have a question, send an e-mail and you will get an answer in a few days. If you have a question and don't have access to the Internet, write to:

Walt Disney World
Box 10000
Lake Buena Vista, FL 32830

COUNTDOWN
TO WALT DISNEY WORLD

10

Start to plan a Disney dinner party. Select favorite vacation foods like hot dogs and ice cream for the menu. Who is on your guest list?

_____
_____
_____

9 DAYS TILL DISNEY

Get to work on your Magic Kingdom Simple Schedule. (Read page 12 to learn how.)

Which ride are you going to go on first?

_____

6

Make some Mouse ears—Tape strips of paper together to make a loop big enough to fit around your head. Then cut out two circles and tape them to the front of the loop. Make a pair for everyone invited to your party.

5 MORE DAYS

Plan your Disney-MGM Studios Simple Schedule. The first two should be almost done by now!

And start packing! (Flip to page 13 for some packing tips.

2 DAYS TO GO!

It's party time! Set the table to look festive for your special Disney dinner party. After dessert, share your theme park schedules with your family. Remember to wear your Mouse ears!

1 DAY LEFT

Don't stay up too late— tomorrow is the big day!

Take a look at a calendar. On which day does your Walt Disney World vacation begin? Once you find it, count back ten days—that's the day you can start this special countdown.

To do it, simply color in the number for each day as it arrives. Then try the daily activity. You can make up your own special activities, too!

8 DAYS LEFT

Make a list with the address of everyone you want to send a postcard to. (Don't forget about e-mail addresses for Internet postcards, too!)

7

It's time to start your Epcot Simple Schedule. Have you finished your Magic Kingdom schedule yet?

Which Epcot ride do you think sounds best? _____

4 DAYS

Pop some popcorn and watch your favorite Disney movie with your family.

Which flick did you pick?
_____

3

Spend some time on your Animal Kingdom Simple Schedule tonight. Finish up schedules for the other parks, too. Which theme park are you going to visit first?_____

Today's the day:

MONTH/DAY/YEAR

You're going to Walt Disney World!

Magic Kingdom

READER
Favorite
Theme
Park
PLEASER

When most people hear the words Walt Disney World, they think of Cinderella Castle, Space Mountain, and, of course, Mickey Mouse. They are all here in the Magic Kingdom, along with much more. That's why so many kids say the Magic Kingdom is the most special part of the World.

You can spend lots of time in its seven lands—Main Street, U.S.A., Adventureland, Frontierland, Liberty Square, Fantasyland, Mickey's Toontown Fair, and Tomorrowland. This chapter will help you decide which attractions you want to see first. Then flip back to page 12. It has tips on how to make a simple Magic Kingdom schedule. That way you can organize your visit and avoid wasting precious time.

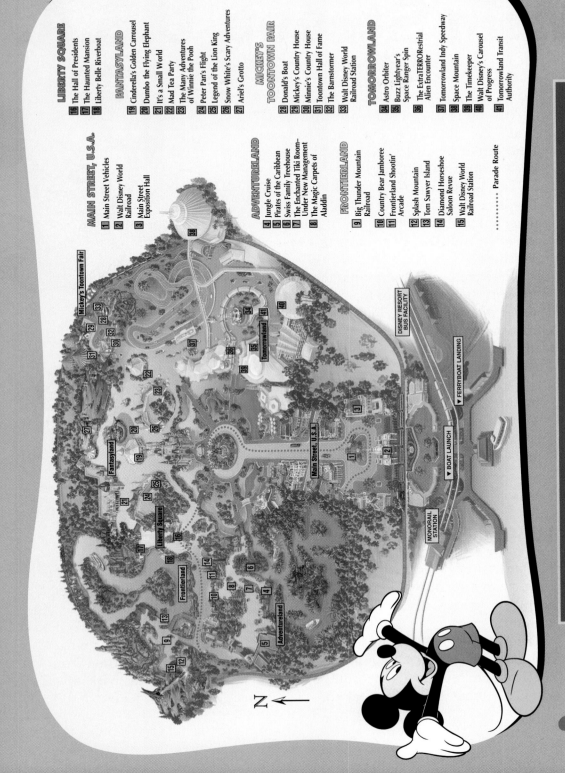

MAIN STREET, U.S.A.
1 Main Street Vehicles
2 Walt Disney World Railroad
3 Main Street Exposition Hall

ADVENTURELAND
4 Jungle Cruise
5 Pirates of the Caribbean
6 Swiss Family Treehouse
7 The Enchanted Tiki Room— Under New Management
8 The Magic Carpets of Aladdin

FRONTIERLAND
9 Big Thunder Mountain Railroad
10 Country Bear Jamboree
11 Frontierland Shootin' Arcade
12 Splash Mountain
13 Tom Sawyer Island
14 Diamond Horseshoe Saloon Revue
15 Walt Disney World Railroad Station

·········· Parade Route

LIBERTY SQUARE
16 The Hall of Presidents
17 The Haunted Mansion
18 Liberty Belle Riverboat

FANTASYLAND
19 Cinderella's Golden Carrousel
20 Dumbo the Flying Elephant
21 It's a Small World
22 Mad Tea Party
23 The Many Adventures of Winnie the Pooh
24 Peter Pan's Flight
25 Legend of the Lion King
26 Snow White's Scary Adventures
27 Ariel's Grotto

MICKEY'S TOONTOWN FAIR
28 Donald's Boat
29 Mickey's Country House
30 Minnie's Country House
31 Toontown Hall of Fame
32 The Barnstormer
33 Walt Disney World Railroad Station

TOMORROWLAND
34 Astro Orbiter
35 Buzz Lightyear's Space Ranger Spin
36 The ExtraTERRORestrial Alien Encounter
37 Tomorrowland Indy Speedway
38 Space Mountain
39 The Timekeeper
40 Walt Disney's Carousel of Progress
41 Tomorrowland Transit Authority

You can get a bigger map of the Magic Kingdom at the park. They're free!

Main Street, U.S.A.

Magic Kingdom

Are you ready for some time traveling? You'll do a lot of it in the Magic Kingdom. Four out of its seven lands send you either back or forward in time.

Main Street, U.S.A., is one of those lands. It was made to look like a small American town in the year 1900. (Some of it is based on the town Walt Disney grew up in—Marceline, Missouri.)

There are pretty lampposts, horse-drawn trolleys, and many other touches that make the street charming. If you look both ways before crossing, you'll notice a big difference between this Main Street and a real one: There's a castle at the end of it!

There are no major rides or attractions here, but Main Street, U.S.A., is still a fun place to be. You can sink your teeth into a fresh-baked cookie, hop aboard a train, or sit on the curb and watch a parade go by.

READER TIP

"The stores on Main Street stay open after the rest of the park closes!"

Greta (age 11)
Brewster, MA

Walt Disney World Railroad

Walt Disney loved trains. He even had a miniature one in his backyard that was big enough for him to ride on.

The Magic Kingdom trains are real locomotives that were built nearly a hundred years ago. A full trip takes about 20 minutes, but you can get on or off at any station (at Main Street, U.S.A., Frontierland, or Mickey's Toontown Fair).

What do the kids who worked on this book think about the railroad? They love traveling by train. You get a great view of the park—plus a chance to rest your feet.

Hot Tip

The names of important Disney workers are written on the windows of Main Street buildings. Look for Walt's name above the ice cream shop.

Hidden Mickey Alert!
Look closely at the horse's bridle gear when you ride the Main Street Trolley.

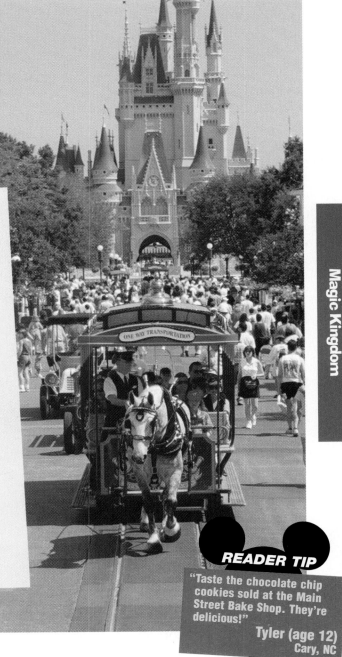

Main Street Vehicles

The Walt Disney World Railroad isn't the only transportation on Main Street, U.S.A. Horse-drawn trolleys, old-fashioned cars, and an antique fire engine make trips up and down the street throughout the day.

You can climb aboard any one of these vehicles in Town Square or by Cinderella Castle. Each trip is strictly one-way—you'll be asked to hop off after the ride.

The vehicles don't operate every day. Stop by City Hall (it's on Main Street) to find out when they are running.

When the horses that pull the trolleys are taking a break, you'll usually find them in the Car Barn near the Emporium. Drop in for a visit.

Hidden Mickey Alert!
Look by the railing around the statue of Walt Disney and Mickey Mouse at the end of Main Street—it casts a Mickey shadow!

READER TIP
"Taste the chocolate chip cookies sold at the Main Street Bake Shop. They're delicious!"
Tyler (age 12)
Cary, NC

Magic Kingdom

19

Adventureland

A trip to Adventureland is like a visit to a tropical island. It has so many plants and trees that George of the Jungle would feel right at home. (Don't bother looking for him. He prefers his own treehouse to the one here. Besides, he probably couldn't find it if he tried.)

As you can tell from the name of this land, the attractions take you on exciting (and silly) adventures.

Hidden Mickey Alert!

As you enter Adventureland, notice the shields above the bridge. One has a Mickey head carved into it.

Jungle Cruise

It's a good thing elephants aren't shy. Otherwise, they might get upset when you watch them take a bath. That's just one of the interesting sights on the Jungle Cruise.

The voyage goes through the jungles of Africa and Asia. Along the way you see life-like zebras, giraffes, lions, hippos, and a few headhunters. (Don't worry—the only real animals in the ride are the humans inside the boat!)

If you love corny jokes, you'll definitely love this ride. The captain tells a bunch of them.

Some kids wish the ride were more exciting. "I love the ride," says Robert. "But it would be even cooler if the headhunters threw their spears."

The Jungle Cruise is usually very crowded—try to get there early in the morning. It's best to ride during the day, when you can see everything.

Hidden Mickey Alert!

Keep an eye out for the bathing elephants—a Mickey is carved into the rock behind them.

LINE GAMES

Search the room with a careful eye to find this mounted butterfly.

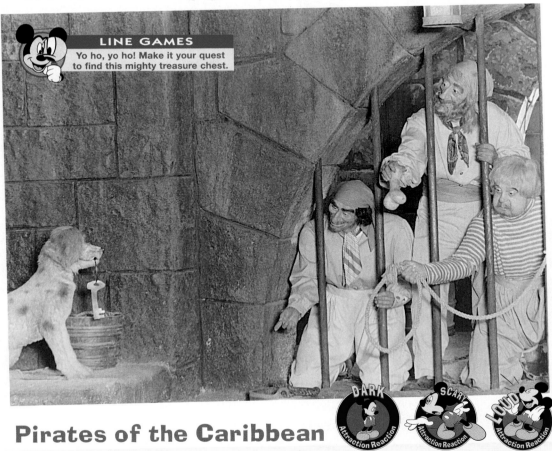

LINE GAMES
Yo ho, yo ho! Make it your quest to find this mighty treasure chest.

Magic Kingdom

Pirates of the Caribbean

Ahoy, there, maties! There's rough waters ahead! That's the warning a pirate gives near the start of this attraction. He must be a wimpy pirate, because kids don't think this ride is rough at all. (But there is a small dip and some dark scenes, so be prepared.)

The journey takes place in a little boat. After floating through a quiet cave ... *BOOM!* You're in the middle of a pirate attack! Cannons blast while the song "Yo Ho, Yo Ho; a Pirate's Life for Me" plays over and over again. Watch for a pirate with his leg hanging over a bridge— the leg is really hairy.

Most kids give the pirates a thumbs-up. "This ride is fun for kids of all ages," says David G. Eric thinks "little kids might be scared. Especially if they aren't ready for the drop." Grace agrees. "The cannons and fire might be too scary, because everything looks so realistic, but that's what I like about it," she says.

HOT TIP

Sit in the front if you want to control how high or low the carpet flies. Back seat drivers are in charge of the side-to-side movements.

The Magic Carpets of Aladdin

If a genie granted you three wishes, what would they be? To be a prince and win the heart of a lovely princess? Well, that was Aladdin's wish, and thanks to his funny friend Genie, his request came true.

You won't find a real genie in this brand-new ride (it's opening in the Spring of 2001), but you will get to take a high flying trip on a magic carpet—just like Aladdin and Jasmine did in the movie.

The magic touch

Like Dumbo the Flying Elephant in Fantasyland, riders on The Magic Carpets of Aladdin use gears to control their own carpet's flight. But unlike Dumbo, these magic carpets really soar! You can also make the carpet move side to side for an especially wild ride.

A whole new world

Kids who made a visit to Adventureland before may notice that this land now has a whole new look. The different shops and decorations make it look just like the busy marketplace of Agrabah from *Aladdin*. You may even see the characters from the movie during your visit. So keep a pen handy for autographs when you're in the area.

Swiss Family Treehouse

Before he wrote a book called The Swiss Family Robinson, Johann Wyss and his kids imagined what it would be like for their family to be stranded on an island. Together they came up with lots of crazy adventures for the Robinsons. They survive a shipwreck, fight off pirates, and build the most awesome treehouse in the world.

Walt Disney Productions made a movie based on the book in 1960.

The Swiss Family Treehouse in Adventureland looks just like the treehouse in the film. In it, you climb a staircase to many different levels. Each room has lots to see. The tree itself looks very real, but it's not. It has 300,000 plastic leaves, and concrete roots.

The Enchanted Tiki Room— Under New Management

Hidden Mickey Alert!
Look for a Mickey or two on the bird perches inside the Tiki Room.

Birds rule at this attraction. They also sing and crack lots of jokes. If you've been here before, you may know José, Michael, Fritz, and Pierre. They've been singing old favorites, like "The Tiki, Tiki, Tiki Room," for more than 25 years.

Now the Tikis are "Under New Management." They have a new show and new bosses. One is Iago, who's as loud and cranky as he was in *Aladdin*. The other is the very nervous Zazu from *The Lion King*. Thanks to Iago, Zazu has plenty to worry about in this musical show.

Frontierland

Howdy, pardners! And welcome to the Wild West. Frontierland shows you what America was like when pioneers first settled west of the Mississippi River. It's also where you'll find two of the best rides in the Magic Kingdom. Both of them are special Disney mountains. You can take a watery trip down Splash Mountain and ride a runaway train at Big Thunder Mountain Railroad. These are just a few of the fun things to do here.

Splash Mountain

After riding Splash Mountain, you'll know how it got its name. It's impossible to stay dry! There are three small dips leading up to a giant, watery drop.

You're all wet

Jennifer B. loves getting wet. That's why she likes to sit in the front seat when she rides Splash Mountain. "You *will* get wet,

especially if you ride up front," she says. You don't get as soaked in the back, but "you feel airborne," Kirsti says.

The scenery tells a story

Kids agree that you have to go on it a few times before you can understand the ride's story. (You travel through scenes from Walt Disney's movie *Song of the South*.) Lindsay says, "Every time there's a little splash, something different

LINE GAMES

Put your thinking cap to use
to find this portrait of Brer Goose.

HoT TiP

If you sit in the front or
on the right side of the
log, you get really wet!

Hidden Mickey Alert!
Look in the clouds during
the final riverboat scene
for a sleeping Mickey.
(It comes after the big
splash.)

READER TIP

"Sometimes the crowd on the
bridge by Splash Mountain
gets splashed, too. It's a
great way to cool off!"

Kate (age 12)
Dearborn, MI

happens to Brer
Rabbit." Brad says,
"Brer Rabbit is supposed to be
in the log getting away from
the fox and the bear." When the
rabbit goes over the edge
toward the end, you go along
for the ride. (Try to keep your
eyes open during the big drop—
it won't be easy.)

Tate thinks that following
the story "makes the ride even
better." Karyn agrees. "All the
characters are so cute and so
detailed, and of course, the last
drop is great."

You must be at least 40 inches
tall to ride.

Magic Kingdom

Country Bear Jamboree

You've never seen bears quite like these. They sing songs, play instruments, and tell jokes. This is a silly show, so be sure to go in with a silly attitude. Big Al is one of the most popular bears. And he can't even carry a tune!

Everyone gets in on the act

Sometimes the audience sings and claps along with the performers. Even the furry heads on the wall get into the act. (Melvin the moose, Buff the buffalo, and Buck the deer like to *hang* around the theater.)

What do kids think of the bears?

The country music show gets mixed reviews from kids. Some love it. Others aren't so thrilled. "It's a good show for little kids," says Eric.

Karyn agrees, saying she would rather spend her time on other rides. "But I think some kids would like to sing along with the characters," she adds.

Brian L. thinks "the bears are great, and some of them are funny. The one that can't sing is really funny. It's a very enjoyable show."

Hot Tip

Tom Sawyer Island is quiet, but it's still rockin'— Teeter-Totter rock is a fun surprise to search for.

Tom Sawyer Island

There's only one way to get to Tom Sawyer Island—by raft. That's the way Tom himself used to travel. (He is a character created by the author Mark Twain.)

Don't expect to find any rides here. In fact, compared to the rest of the Magic Kingdom, it's a pretty calm place. But if you bring your imagination, you can have exciting adventures of your own.

Bouncy bridges and secret exits

The island has a real windmill to wander through, hills to climb, and two neat bridges. One of them is an old barrel bridge. When one person bounces on it, everyone does.

Across one bridge is a big fort. An Audio-Animatronic blacksmith is working inside it. And there's a secret exit that is really a path through a dark and narrow cave.

In all, there are three caves to explore. They are the best things on the island. Beware: The caves are very dark and a little scary.

Younger kids love it here

All of Tom Sawyer Island is popular with younger kids. Older kids think the bridges and caves are the best part.

If you get hungry, stop by Aunt Polly's Dockside Inn for a snack. The pickles are delicious!

Magic Kingdom

Who am I?

- My nose is always itchy
- All my clothes are super small
- Heigh ho, it's off to work I go!

Answer: Sneezy

Hidden Mickey Alert!

This Hidden Mickey is a prickly one—it's part of a cactus at Big Thunder's exit.

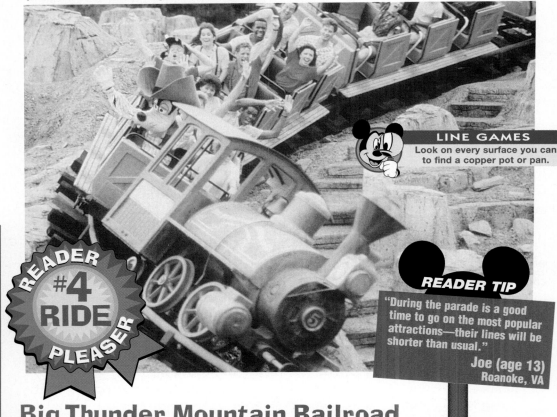

LINE GAMES
Look on every surface you can to find a copper pot or pan.

#4 RIDE
READER PLEASER

READER TIP
"During the parade is a good time to go on the most popular attractions—their lines will be shorter than usual."
Joe (age 13)
Roanoke, VA

Big Thunder Mountain Railroad

Hang on to your hat, because this is one of the wildest rides in the wilderness. The speedy trains zip in, out, and over a huge mountain. They pass through scenes with real-looking chickens, goats, donkeys, and more.

A calmer coaster

The swoops and turns make this a thrilling roller coaster, but it's a lot tamer than Space Mountain. It's a ride you can go on again and again, and see new things each time. Look for funny sights in the town—like the poor guy floating around in a bathtub. Try to ride during the day and again at night.

Scream your head off

Kids have good things to say about this ride. "There are lots of fast turns and drops," says Jennifer B. Justin says, "It's not too scary, but I was screaming because it's so much fun." David G. agrees. "I just love screaming and putting my hands in the air during the dips," he says.

You must be at least 40 inches tall to ride.

ROUGH Attraction Reaction

Who am I?

- I can't find my shadow
- I don't want to grow up
- I can fly! I can fly! I can fly!

Answer: Peter Pan

More Frontierland Fun!

At the **Frontierland Shootin' Arcade**, you can aim air rifles at targets like tombstones and skulls. (You have to pay extra to use the arcade. It's not included in your Magic Kingdom park admission.)

Nearby, a crew of singers and dancers performs all day at the **Diamond Horseshoe Saloon Revue**. The jokes are silly, but the show is a lot of fun. Sometimes people from the audience can even be in the show. If you want to get in on the act, sit near the front. If you have stage fright, it's best to watch from the balcony!

HOTEL

GENERAL STORE

SCHOOL

JAIL

Liberty Square

What did America look like in colonial days? Parts of it looked like Liberty Square! This small area separates Frontierland from Fantasyland. It's a quiet spot with some shops and a couple of popular attractions.

Magic Kingdom

The Haunted Mansion

This haunted house isn't too scary, but there are plenty of ghosts to keep you on your toes. Before you enter, read the funny tombstones in the graveyard outside. (We love the one that says: Here lies good old Fred. A great big rock fell on his head.)

Once inside, you'll be stranded in a room with no windows and no doors. For a while, it seems like there's no way out.

You are doomed

There's a moment before you board your "Doom Buggy" when the room is totally dark. It only lasts a few seconds, but for some, it's much too long.

The car doesn't move very fast, but it's still hard to catch all of the details. Watch for the big door knockers that knock by themselves, a ghostly teapot pouring tea, and a ghost napping under the table at a party in the ballroom.

Fun for everyone

This ride is popular with people of all ages. Some parts are spooky, but in a fun way. Just ask Eric. "I was tense because it was my first time, but it wasn't that scary after all," he says.

LINE GAMES
Swiftly scout the graveyard park to find this stone for Grandpa Marc.

The Hall of Presidents

The first part of this attraction is a film about our government. Then the screen rises and all of the American presidents are on stage together. They are Audio-Animatronics, but they look real. Can you find Bill Clinton in the photo above?

Bill Clinton and Abraham Lincoln actually speak. (Mr. Clinton recorded the voice himself. Abraham Lincoln's voice is performed by an actor.) If you watch closely, you'll notice the presidents move, whisper, and even doze off.

The kids were pleasantly surprised by this attraction. Danielle G. says, "I thought it would be boring, but it isn't." Lindsay agrees. "It's a fun way to learn," she says.

Liberty Belle Riverboat

The Liberty Belle Riverboat docks in Liberty Square. This big steamboat takes guests on slow, relaxing cruises. It can be a nice break on a hot day. The best seats are right up front or in the back, where you can see both sides of the river as you float along.

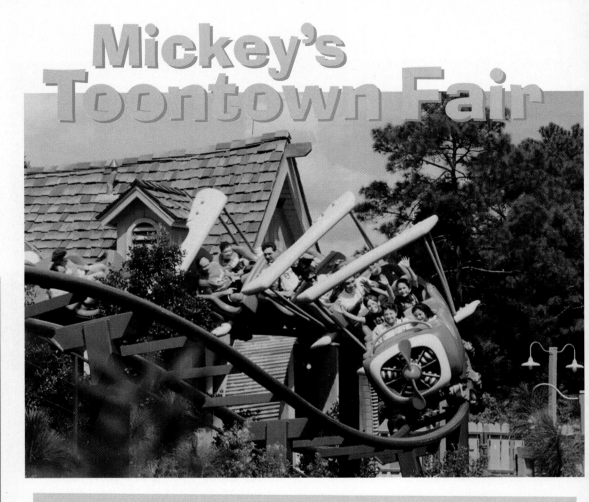

Mickey's Toontown Fair

Are you looking for that world-famous mouse? You're sure to find him at Mickey's Toontown Fair. He has a job here and, of course, he does it well.

This is the newest land in the Magic Kingdom. It must be a great place because Mickey, Minnie, and their friends all have country homes here. Everywhere you look, you see colorful tents. That's because the county fair is always in town. Guess who's the head judge. (Hint: Think of the mouse who does a good job.)

To get here, follow the path from the Mad Tea Party or from Space Mountain. Or take a ride on the Walt Disney World Railroad. It's a short trip and, if you ask Michael, it's worth it. "I think all kids will like it here," he says.

The Barnstormer

The only ride in Toontown Fair is the roller coaster at Goofy's Wiseacre Farm. The ride may look small, but it packs plenty of thrills. "I like the part where you go sideways really fast," Szasha says.

During the trip a plane takes you on a wild tour of Goofy's farm. It starts out slow, but watch out! You're about to crash into Goofy's barn. The hole in the wall tells you that someone has been there before you. Yes, it's clumsy old Goofy.

Before you ride The Barnstormer spend some time exploring Goofy's farm. Some of his vegetables are pretty wacky, just like him. (Can you spot the "bell" peppers?) Then look up. Only Goofy would park his airplane in a water tower!

Magic Kingdom

LINE GAMES
Study the farm that Goofy's cropped to find this corn that's already popped.

Donald's Boat

A popular stop in Toontown is Donald's Boat. It's called the *Miss Daisy* and it's full of leaks. When you pull the whistle, water shoots out the top. To get to the boat, cross the "duck pond"— another great spot to get wet.

READER TIP
"The Barnstormer isn't just for little kids. It's loads of fun!"
Richard (age 13)
Cooper City, FL

Hot Tip
Mickey's Toontown Fair is a great place to meet the characters.

33

Hidden Mickey Alert!
In Toontown the Mickeys are
practically everywhere! Look
for them on plants, benches,
lampposts, and windows.

Mickey's Country House

The door is open, so come on in!
Mickey's country house tells you a
lot about him. His game room is
full of sports stuff. But the kitchen
is a mess. That must be what
happens when you let Donald
and Goofy decorate!

Where's Mickey? He's hard at
work in the Judge's Tent. Walk out
the back door of the house and
follow the path. You can't miss it!
On your way, check out Mickey's
garden. Even the vegetables have
Mouse ears.

Judge's Tent

You found him! Mickey is here
all day long, ready to have his
picture taken with you. There's
always a long wait, but the line
is shorter late in the day.

Minnie's Country House

Go ahead, climb on the
furniture—Minnie won't mind.
There's lots to see and touch in
this house. Press the button on
Minnie's answering machine and
listen to her messages. Open the
refrigerator, and feel the cold air.
And get set for a trick when you
try to take a chocolate chip cookie
off her table.

Grace thinks younger kids will
love Minnie's house "because
there's so much to do. You can play
with everything in her kitchen. I
like the microwave oven!" she says.

Once you've explored inside, head
for Minnie's backyard. She is a very
good gardener. On your way there,
look at the funny flowers in the sun
room. The palm tree has hands, the
tiger lilies have tiger faces, and the
tulips all have two lips!

Toontown Hall of Fame

This tent is filled with winning
entries from the fair and goodies
to buy. But the best reason to
come here is to meet Disney
characters. They are hanging out
in three different rooms. You have
to stand in a separate line to enter
each room. The sign shows which
characters are in each room, so
you can pick which line to get in.

Magic Kingdom

34

EXTRA! EXTRA! THE TOONS ARE MAKING NEWS!

They need your help to finish the article. Fill in the blanks below with the kind of word that is missing—a noun, adjective, verb, or exclamation. Then read the finished sentences to get the scoop.

Cartoon Tribune

Early this morning the residents of Toontown awoke to
_____ shouts coming from the _____
　　　ADJECTIVE　　　　　　　　　　　　　　　　　NOUN
store. "Thief! Thief!" yelled the store owner. "Somebody stole
my _____ _____."
　　　ADJECTIVE　　　　NOUN

All of the town's toons ran over to help catch the crooks.
They searched up the streets and down the streets, and behind
every _____ and _____, but not one
　　　　NOUN　　　　　　　　　NOUN
thief was found.

"I haven't had any luck so far," sighed Minnie. All I
found was a _____ _____."
　　　　　　　ADJECTIVE　　　　NOUN

The store owner started to _____. "It was
　　　　　　　　　　　　　　　　VERB
my favorite," he said. "Without it, I won't be able to _____."
　　　　　　　　　　　　　　　　　　　　　　　　　　　　　VERB

Hearing that gave Goofy an idea. "What were you doing when you saw it last?" he asked.

"If I remember correctly I was about to _____, because I was feeling very
　　　　　　　　　　　　　　　　　　　VERB
_____."
ADJECTIVE

"A-HA!" declared Goofy triumphantly. "Then all we have to do is look by the _____
　　　　　　　　　　　　　　　　　　　　　　　　　　　　　　　　　　　　ADJECTIVE
_____ in your shop, and what's missing will soon be found." Goofy began to
NOUN
_____ toward the shop and all the toons followed in wonder. When they got to the
VERB
_____, they couldn't believe their eyes.
NOUN

"_____ !" the shop owner shouted. "Now I can _____ again!"
　EXCLAMATION　　　　　　　　　　　　　　　　　　　　　　VERB

"Hooray for Goofy," everyone cheered. "He saved the day!"

The store owner was so pleased that he decided to put a portrait of Goofy in his shop, so
no one will ever forget how wise the Goof can be.

35

Fantasyland

Fantasyland is home to a lot of magical rides that younger kids just love. Older kids and even grown-ups enjoy them, too. These attractions are very popular, and the waits can be long. But the lines are usually shorter while people are watching the afternoon parade. So it's a good idea to skip the parade one day and spend time in Fantasyland. Plan to catch the parade on another day.

Ariel's Grotto

There is a mysterious blue cave tucked behind Dumbo the Flying Elephant. Inside, there is a special surprise—and her name is Ariel. The star of *The Little Mermaid* is waiting to meet you in her grotto (grotto is another word for cave). Ask her to sign the autograph section that starts on page 158.

Out front, there are some fountains to play in, so it's a great place to get wet.

Szasha says, "If you really like Ariel, you should definitely go." She also likes the "funny rocks that squirt water." Danielle T. has this advice: "Try to go when it's not so crowded, or you may have to wait a long time."

Hot Tip

Belle from Beauty and the Beast sometimes reads stories and signs autographs in Fairy Tale Garden by Cinderella Castle. Check a park guidemap to see what time she'll appear during your visit.

Cinderella's Golden Carrousel

Just about all of the attractions at Walt Disney World were dreamed up by Disney Imagineers. But not the carousel. It was discovered in New Jersey, where it was once part of another amusement park. It was built around 1917.

When you climb on a horse for your ride on the carousel, be sure to notice that each one is different. And remember to look up at the ceiling and its hand-painted scenes from *Cinderella*. While you ride, enjoy famous Disney tunes, including "Zip-A-Dee-Doo-Dah," "When You Wish Upon a Star," and "Be Our Guest."

The kids all enjoy a spin on Disney's carousel. "You can never grow too old for a carousel," says Lissy. "The horses are beautiful and the music makes it great." Robert agrees. "I love the carousel. I think people of any age would like it."

Mad Tea Party

The idea for the giant teacups that spin through this ride came from a famous scene in *Alice in Wonderland*. In the movie, the Mad Hatter throws himself a tea party to celebrate his un-birthday. That's any day of the year that isn't his birthday!

You control the spin

On the Mad Tea Party ride, you control how fast your cup spins by turning the big wheel in the center. The more you turn, the more you spin. Or you can just sit back and let the cup spin on its own. It may be hard while you're whirling, but try to take a peek at the little mouse who keeps popping out of the big teapot in the center.

"It's a very good ride and it really makes you dizzy," says Nita. Brian L. agrees. "I wish it would

Hot Tip

Sometimes the characters from Alice in Wonderland join guests for a spin in their teacup!

go even faster, but it's good that you spin as fast or as slow as you want," he says.

It takes teamwork

For the best ride, David B. suggests that everyone in the cup try to work together. "You have to coordinate," he says. "Sometimes you can go faster if fewer people work at spinning the wheel."

Most kids agree that the ride is too short (it lasts about two minutes). Lissy doesn't mind, though. "Your arms get tired after a while," says Lissy, "but the teacups are always fun."

READER TIP

"There is always a mad rush for Dumbo, so get there very early!"
Jessica (age 12)
Staten Island, NY

Magic Kingdom

Dumbo the Flying Elephant

Just like the star of the movie *Dumbo*, these elephants know how to fly. They'd love to take you for a short ride (about two minutes) above Fantasyland. A button lets you control the up and down movement of the elephant.

Take your kid brother

Many of the kids agree that this ride is more fun for younger kids from ages 3 to 8. But they all find something to like, and think it would be fun to go on with a younger brother or sister.

Brian L. also suggests it for younger kids. "It's not a bad ride,

and I think little kids would love it," he says. Robert likes "to go up really high. I think some kids might be scared of the height, though."

Beware of long lines

Even though Disney added more Dumbos a few years ago, lines for this attraction tend to be long. Anna thinks the ride is "way too short. But if you don't wait in line too long, it's fun to go on."

Danielle G. loves it. "It has the appearance of a child's ride, but it's fun for everyone," she says. Tate agrees. "Most people think it's just for little kids, but I think it's fun."

LINE GAMES
When you're in line, make it your goal to find this painted totem pole.

Peter Pan's Flight

DARK
Attraction Reaction

Swoop and soar through scenes that tell the story of how Wendy, Michael, and John get sprinkled with pixie dust and fly off to Never Land with Peter Pan and Tinker Bell. Along the way you meet up with Princess Tiger Lily, the evil Captain Hook, and his sidekick Mr. Smee.

Near the beginning of the trip, there's a beautiful scene of London at night. Notice that the cars on the streets really move. Later, watch out for the crocodile who wants to eat Captain Hook.

When you first board your pirate ship, it seems like you're riding on a track on the ground. Once you get going the track is actually above you, so it feels like the ship is really flying.

"I love this ride and how it makes you feel like you can fly," says Robert. "I especially like the part at the end with the crocodile."

Jennifer B. thinks "it's fun to look down at London below and see all the small cars and bright city lights."

David B. points out that Peter Pan's Flight is different from all the other Fantasyland rides because "you're hooked from the top instead of being on a track below you." He adds, "I never get tired of this ride."

Hidden Mickey Alert!
Many Mickeys can be found in the vines you see in the African scene.

LINE GAMES
Look for objects that won't stay still to find this whirling swirling mill.

It's a Small World

People have a lot in common, no matter where they live. That's the point of this attraction. In it, you take a slow boat ride through several large rooms where singing dolls represent different parts of the world. There are Greek dancers, Japanese kite flyers, Scottish bagpipers, and many more. There's also a jungle scene with hippos, giraffes, and monkeys.

All this colorful scenery is set to the song "It's a Small World." Pay attention to the costumes on the dolls, and try to guess which country they're from. Nita says,

"The costumes are adorable, and I like the faces on the dolls. But the ride is too slow. If it had a few dips, it would be better."

David G. does think the ride is "slow moving, but it's fun at the same time." Jennifer B. agrees. "It's a nice, relaxing boat ride after a long day in the theme parks," she says.

It's a Small World is loved by people of all ages. That's why it's one of the most famous rides in Walt Disney World. As Eric sums it up: "I would hope that everyone likes it, even if the song is a little bit repetitive!"

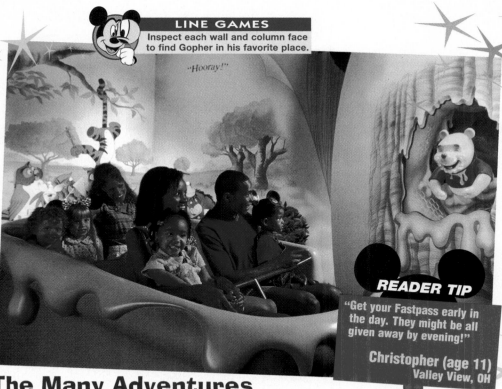

"Hooray!"

READER TIP

"Get your Fastpass early in
the day. They might be all
given away by evening!"

Christopher (age 11)
Valley View, OH

The Many Adventures
of Winnie the Pooh

Winnie the Pooh loves his honey. In fact, he'll do anything to keep the sweet treat safe. On this dizzying trip through the Hundred Acre Wood, see what Pooh must do to rescue his honey pots and his friends, too.

The blustery day

The wind is howling, the leaves are rustling, and everything in Pooh's world is blowing away. Roo and Piglet are up in the air. Even Owl's house is about to topple over. You better hang on to your honey pot, or you just might be swept off next!

A sticky situation

Finally the wind calms and Pooh can get to sleep. But when he wakes up from his silly dream, it's raining outside. Pooh's honey pots are about to wash away. He can save them, but will he save himself?

Everyone loves Pooh

Adam P. thinks "everyone will like this ride." Leah agrees, but adds, "I think little kids would like it best." Jennifer S. says, "All of the special effects were really neat. It really looked like it was raining." Nicholas has a favorite effect, too. "I liked the part when we bounced with Tigger." What's your favorite?

Honey Hunt

Winnie the Pooh has lost ten pots of honey and he doesn't know what to do. Use the clues below to help Pooh figure out which words his precious pots are hiding in. (*Hint*: You can use the color key to fill in some or all of the missing letters in the answers!)

POOH'S CLUES

POOH'S ANSWERS

1. Vegetable . . . . P O T ☐ ☐ ☐

2. Mrs. Potts . . . . ☐ ☐ ☐ P O T

3. Tubby tummy. . . . . P O T ☐ ☐ ☐ ☐ ☐

4. Clay vases . . . . P O T ☐ ☐ ☐ ☐

5. Completely clean . . . . ☐ P O T ☐ ☐ ☐ ☐

6. Big dent in the street . . . . P O T ☐ ☐ ☐

7. Plant holder . . . . ☐ ☐ ☐ ☐ ☐ ☐ P O T

8. Woody and
   Buzz's buddy . . . ☐ ☐ . P O T ☐ ☐ ☐ ☐ ☐ ☐ ☐

9. African mammal . . ☐ ☐ ☐ ☐ ☐ P O T ☐ ☐ ☐

10. Meaty main dish . . . . P O T ☐ ☐ ☐ ☐

Color Key

= A	= B	= D	= E	= F	= H
= I	= L	= M	= O	= P	= R
= S	= T	= U	= W	= Y	

Hidden Mickey Alert!

Mickey is hiding on the mural in Snow White's waiting area. He's by the flowers!

LINE GAMES

You don't need a mirror fit for a Queen to find this turtle that's painted green.

DARK
Attraction Reaction

SCARY
Attraction Reaction

Snow White's Scary Adventures

This attraction takes you through scenes from the movie *Snow White and the Seven Dwarfs*. Some scenes are sweet, while others are scary. If you like Snow White, you're in luck. She is in a lot of scenes (but so is the nasty old witch). Don't expect to see much of the dwarfs—they don't show up a lot.

There are lots of turns, and the witch seems to be around each one of them. It's very dark during most of the ride, so it can get pretty creepy—especially for younger kids.

The kids aren't sure who this ride is meant for. It's too scary for many small children and a little simple for older kids.

David G. says, "This ride focuses too much on the wicked witch." Grace agrees. "There are not enough scenes of Snow White and the dwarfs. Make sure you look at the warning sign before you get on the ride. It might be very scary for some kids," she adds.

Legend of the Lion King

Disney's hit movie comes to life in Legend of the Lion King. This show uses animation, life-size puppets, special effects, and music to tell the story of Simba and his friends from the movie.

When the sun rises over Pride Rock, Mufasa and Simba make their big entrance. The characters may look life-like, but they are really large puppets.

Sing "Hakuna Matata"

As the story continues, other characters act out parts of the movie. Special effects, like a soft wind and flashes of lightning, make the storm seem real. During the stampede scene, the room rumbles. Of course, no Lion King show would be complete without a visit from Timon and Pumbaa. When they sing "Hakuna Matata," feel free to sing along!

Kids agree

All the kids agree that this is a great show. Jennifer B. thinks that "if you haven't seen the movie, this show is a great way to learn the story." David G. enjoys the show because it "combines live action and clips from the movie on stage." Michael just loves everything about it. "It's the best play I've ever seen," he says.

LOUD Attraction Reaction

Hidden Mickey Alert!

Notice the rocks in the Legend of the Lion King theater. They form a Mickey.

Tomorrowland

Tomorrowland began as a peek at the future. But as the real world changed, so did this land. Now, it's like a city from a science fiction story. The palm trees are made of metal. The rides here let you rocket through space or travel through time. And a scary alien even beams down for a visit! A good way to see this land is to ride on the Tomorrowland Transit Authority—it's cool and breezy, and it never has a long line.

Hidden Mickey Alert!

This Hidden Mickey is from outer space! When three meteors crash on the ceiling of Space Mountain, they form a giant Mickey head.

Space Mountain

Thrill seekers like to head straight for this rocket ride through outer space. It has twists, turns, and a few steep dips. And it all takes place in the dark! Space Mountain is one of the most popular rides in Walt Disney World.

Older kids love it

Danielle T. says, "I really felt like I was in a rocket going to space. This is one of the best rides." Jennifer B. agrees. "I like how it's

READER #2 RIDE PLEASER

all in the dark. The suspense makes it so much fun."

Nita has a warning: "It goes too fast. I'm not a roller coaster person, and I felt like I was about to fall out."

Is it too scary?

Everyone agrees: Space Mountain is scary! But some kids say it's a "good scary." Anything that was "bad scary" happened only in their imaginations.

Anna says, "The ride rattles a lot. I wish that there were higher sides to the cars." But don't worry: The coaster is perfectly safe. And, as David G. says, "Space Mountain is a must for all roller coaster fans!" Is it for you?

You must be at least 44 inches tall to ride.

Magic Kingdom

LINE GAMES
No shuttle is needed, or crew to man it, to find a galaxy or planet.

Hidden Mickey Alert!
While in line for this attraction, look for a Mickey hiding in the alien writing on the wall.

HoT TiP Sit in the front row for the closest—and scariest—encounter.

The ExtraTERRORestrial Alien Encounter

People from another planet want to show off their new machine. They say it can beam people through space. But that's not what happens. Instead, an alien arrives and escapes into the audience. It's ugly and it's hungry. And it just might eat you!

It's not for everyone

That's the story of Alien Encounter, the Magic Kingdom's scariest attraction. Kids like this show a lot but say that it's not for everyone—especially younger kids. "The first time I went on it, I was 10 and I cried," says Amy. "But I've always been a scaredy cat."

Brian F. says, "I did not go on it, because I don't like aliens. I went to the arcade instead." Lindsay feels just the opposite. She likes scary things and loves this attraction.

The alien licks your head

Jennifer B. warns, "Don't be surprised if the alien licks you, breathes on you, or touches you!"

Grace loves the effects. "Sit back in your seat to make sure you can feel the alien when he's behind you," she says. David G. also has a tip: "If you get too scared, just close your eyes!"

You must be at least 44 inches tall to enter Alien Encounter.

LINE GAMES
You don't have to know its definition to find "Hyper Transport" before the mission.

The Timekeeper

Travel through time with Timekeeper, one of the world's wackiest robots. He takes you on a tour of the past and the future.

Okay, you don't *really* get to time travel in this attraction—but it feels like you do. A robot named 9-Eye is the real time traveler. She takes pictures that fill the nine screens in the theater. A movie completely surrounds the audience.

It will make your head spin

When you watch the screens, it feels like you're moving. "This made me dizzy," says Lindsay. "But it still is sort of neat." Eric agrees. "The Timekeeper is really good. I especially liked the end. But don't go if your feet are tired, since there are no seats, only rails to lean on."

Don't miss it

Grace says, "It's so funny that you don't even notice it's educational." Seth has a tip for kids who have never seen it before: "Don't forget to look behind you." Otherwise you might miss something.

Arcade Alert!

The **Tomorrowland Light & Power Co.** is a high-tech video arcade. It's right next to Space Mountain.

It's a good place to wait if you don't want to ride Space Mountain or go to Alien Encounter. Just like other arcades, you have to pay to play here.

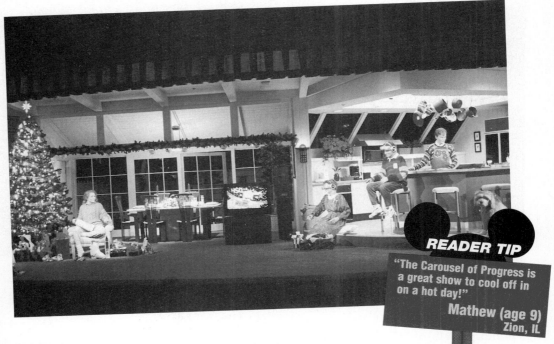

Walt Disney's Carousel of Progress

A lot has changed since 1900. There was no electricity, water came from a well, and nobody had a TV. Life was rough! This attraction shows you how life has changed since then.

A look at American families

The show is called Carousel of Progress because you move in a circle, just like on a carousel. You pass different scenes along the way. Each one teaches a little history.

"I really appreciate the story," says Tate. "It's a down-to-earth look at how the American family has progressed over the years."

Learning can be fun

Anna finds it "a good way to learn. I think it's cool when they say, in the early scenes, how 'that will never happen,' and we know that it already has."

Adam W. likes "how we learn about all the inventions that were created in the years past."

Eric's favorite scene comes at the end. "It's so funny to see Granny playing the virtual reality game. It's neat to watch one family change over time."

What's your favorite scene in the Carousel of Progress?

Hidden Mickey Alert!

Watch the planets carefully as they whiz by. One of them is extra special—it has a Mickey on it!

Hot Tip

To get more points on the Buzz Lightyear ride, hold the button down the whole time, and aim at small, moving, or far away targets.

LINE GAMES

In Buzz's world you can't think small to find this jumbo Magic 8-Ball.

Buzz Lightyear's Space Ranger Spin

In this attraction, everyone is a toy—including you. In fact, you are so small, you fit inside a video game shooting gallery.

Disney's FASTPASS

To infinity and beyond!

The ride is under the command of Buzz Lightyear. You've just become a Junior Space Ranger, so you're under his command, too. Together, you battle the evil Emperor Zurg.

Zap that Zurg

Zurg and his robots are stealing batteries from other toys. They plan to use the batteries to power their ultimate weapon of destruction. Your job is to fight back. Use the laser cannons in your spaceship to aim at the targets (they look like Z's) and zap Zurg's power. Every time you hit a target you earn more points. There is a scoreboard by your cannon that shows you how many points you've gotten. At the end of the ride, you'll pass a giant chart. It shows everyone's ranger rank based on their score. Check to see where your score falls. Most kids improve every time they ride.

Who am I?

- I don't want strings attached
- I made a donkey of myself
- I learned my lesson: never lie!

Answer: Pinocchio

Tomorrowland Indy Speedway

You don't need a license to drive your own car around this racetrack (as long as you're 52 inches tall). Cars travel along a track, but it's not as easy to drive as it looks. Even experts bounce around a lot. The cars are real and are powered by gasoline.

Some of the kids really enjoy driving their own cars. "The race cars are fun because you get to steer them yourself," says Szasha. "I like the curves." Robert says, "I love it. I think it goes pretty fast and I like having my own car."

Karyn thinks the race cars could be a little more exciting. David B. agrees. "I like the ride," he says. "But I wish they didn't have the track in the middle."

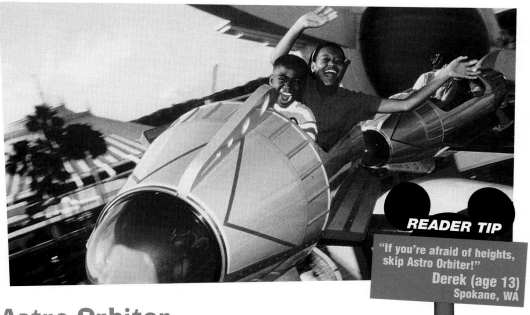

Magic Kingdom

Astro Orbiter

In the middle of Tomorrowland, there is a giant, glowing tower. It is called Rockettower. The Astro Orbiter ride is all the way at the top. In it, you soar past colorful planets high above Tomorrowland.

You can take the ride by yourself or with a friend. (Each rocket fits two people.) "This is a fun ride," says Eric, "and the view is very pretty at night." Dawna thinks, "People who don't have the stomach for Space Mountain can go. It still has the space theme."

Kirsti has a tip: "Sit in the front so you can control how high up you go."

Tomorrowland Transit Authority

This slow-moving ride travels by or through most of Tomorrowland's attractions. If you're not sure about going on Space Mountain, the view from here can help you decide. It's also interesting that the ride doesn't give off any pollution. Szasha says, "It takes you past the different rides so you can see what they are like before riding them." This is Eric's favorite ride. "It gives you a very nice, relaxing tour of Tomorrowland," he says. Michael adds, "The announcer tells you about each ride. And it's a good place to rest your feet."

Entertainment

The Magic Kingdom is a very entertaining place. It seems like there is always a show starting or a parade going by. Read on to learn about some of the special events that take place in the park. For more information, check a park guidemap. You can get one in any Disney resort, at the entrance to the park, or in the shops and restaurants.

SPECTROMAGIC

This parade makes its way down Main Street twice each night during busy seasons. Special lighting effects and lots of characters make for a show that, as Dawna says, "no one should miss. It's the perfect way to end an evening or a trip."

DISNEY'S MAGICAL MOMENTS PARADE

Your favorite Disney characters are on the march in this parade. Mickey and all of his pals want you to join in the fun. Danielle T. says, "I danced in the Cinderella scene. It was an experience I'll never forget!"

Each parade float has a surprise, like confetti or fireworks. Szasha has a tip: "Get a spot on the curb early. They may ask you to be in the parade."

FANTASY IN THE SKY FIREWORKS

Look—up in the sky! It's not a bird or a plane . . . it's the most amazing fireworks show you've ever seen! Hundreds of colorful bursts explode within seven minutes. For the best view of the show, stand right in the middle of Main Street, facing the castle.

Where to find
CHARACTERS
at the MAGIC KINGDOM

Disney characters greet guests all over the Magic Kingdom. The best place to find them is **Mickey's Toontown Fair**. You can meet Mickey in the **Judge's Tent**, and the rest of the gang in the **Toontown Hall of Fame**.

Characters from *The Jungle Book*, *Aladdin*, and *The Lion King* hang out in **Adventureland**. Alice in Wonderland and her friends prefer **Fantasyland**, while Brer Fox and Brer Bear enjoy spending time near **Splash Mountain**.

If you want to meet the Little Mermaid, go to **Ariel's Grotto** in Fantasyland. There are lots of fountains you can play in, too.

To find out exactly where and when to meet your favorite characters, pick up a free park guidemap or ask a cast member.

Magic Kingdom

Head to this park first, since it has the most rides for kids.

Arrive a half hour before the opening time. Walk down Main Street to get a head start for when the rest of the park opens.

Check the Tip Boards on Main Street and in Tomorrowland. They list the wait times for popular attractions.

Rest your feet and watch a movie starring Mickey in the Exposition Hall on Main Street. Afterward, you can e-mail a photo of yourself to a friend or pose for pictures in front of funny backgrounds. Sometimes characters hang out there, too!

Need to cool off on a hot day? You can get soaked at Ariel's Grotto in Fantasyland, Donald's Boat in Mickey's Toontown Fair, or Cool Ship in Tomorrowland.

If the park is open late, it's fun to go on your favorite attractions again after dark.

There are "chicken exits" in the lines for all scary rides, just in case you change your mind about riding at the last minute.

Never eat just before riding The Barnstormer, Astro Orbiter, Space Mountain, Big Thunder Mountain Railroad, or the Mad Tea Party.

If you've never been on a roller coaster, ride The Barnstormer first. If you like it, try Big Thunder Mountain Railroad next. Save Space Mountain for last—it's the scariest.

If there are two lines at an attraction, the one on the left is usually shorter.

Attraction Ratings

COOL
(Check It Out)

- Cinderella's Golden Carrousel
- Snow White's Scary Adventures
- The Hall of Presidents
- The Timekeeper
- Tomorrowland Transit Authority
- Tom Sawyer Island
- Liberty Belle Riverboat
- Swiss Family Treehouse
- The Enchanted Tiki Room—Under New Management

REALLY COOL
(Don't Miss)

- The Barnstormer
- Astro Orbiter
- Tomorrowland Indy Speedway
- Mad Tea Party
- Country Bear Jamboree
- Jungle Cruise
- It's a Small World
- Carousel of Progress
- Walt Disney World Railroad
- Dumbo the Flying Elephant
- The Magic Carpets of Aladdin

THE COOLEST
(See at Least Twice)

- Space Mountain
- Splash Mountain
- Big Thunder Mountain Railroad
- The Haunted Mansion
- Peter Pan's Flight
- Alien Encounter
- Buzz Lightyear's Space Ranger Spin
- Pirates of the Caribbean
- Legend of the Lion King
- The Many Adventures of Winnie the Pooh

What do YOU think?

The kids who worked on this book rated all the attractions at Walt Disney World. But your opinion counts, too! Make your own "Attraction Ratings" list for each park and send it to us. We'll use it when we create next year's book. (Our address is on page 8.)

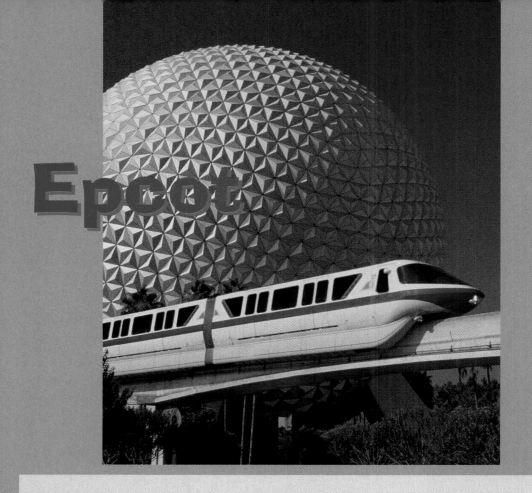

Epcot

Epcot is a great place to make discoveries about the world. At this theme park, things that used to seem ordinary suddenly become fun. All of the attractions at Epcot are in buildings called pavilions. The pavilions are in two sections of the park. One section is Future World, and the other is World Showcase. Future World celebrates cool inventions and ideas. It shows how they affect everything, from the land and sea to your mind and body.

World Showcase lets you travel around the world without leaving the park! There are many different countries to visit here. Each country has copies of its famous buildings, restaurants, and other landmarks. Together, they make you feel as if you're visiting the real place.

WORLD SHOWCASE

MOROCCO

FRANCE

JAPAN

INTERNATIONAL GATEWAY

THE AMERICAN ADVENTURE

UNITED KINGDOM

ITALY

CANADA

FUTURE WORLD

GERMANY

WORLD SHOWCASE LAGOON

IMAGINATION!

THE LAND

CHINA

SHOWCASE PLAZA

INNOVENTIONS WEST

THE LIVING SEAS

NORWAY

INNOVENTIONS EAST

MEXICO

TEST TRACK

SPACESHIP EARTH

To Buses

N

Entrance Plaza

WONDERS OF LIFE

UNIVERSE OF ENERGY

Epcot is a big place. Use this map to help plan your trip through the park.

Future World

When you enter Epcot by monorail, you are in the area called Future World. Many of the attractions here are educational—but that doesn't mean you won't have fun. Take it from other kids: There's a lot to discover.

Epcot

LINE GAMES
Explore each space at every height to find this spinning satellite.

SPACESHIP EARTH

You can't miss the silver ball that is the symbol of Epcot. It's gigantic. The Spaceship Earth ride is inside this big, round building. The ride shows you the different ways people have communicated over the years.

DARK Attraction Reaction

A highlight of the trip is when your time machine vehicle reaches the top of the building. Look up and you'll think you are staring into a night sky. The stars are beautiful.

Leah thinks Spaceship Earth could be a favorite for people interested in history. Adam P. agrees. "I love history, and I liked this ride a lot!"

After the ride, check out the Global Neighborhood. It's full of games and other fun activities that teach you about communication.

Chill out!

Need a place to escape from the heat? Head to Ice Station Cool in Innoventions Plaza. The entrance is an arctic chamber that's so cold it has real snow in it all year long! Inside you can sample sodas from all different countries for free. Some are delicious, but most kids think one tastes terrible. Are you brave enough to sample them all?

HOT TIP

Finding your way around this pavilion is a snap with an Innoventions map. Pick one up at the entrance.

READER TIP

"Watch the sidewalk outside Innoventions at night. It sparkles!"

David (age 7)
Reading, PA

Epcot

INNOVENTIONS

Here's your chance to test out some exciting new inventions. You may also talk on a giant phone, send a video postcard to a friend by e-mail, or learn how to make pancakes from wood pulp.

On the road again

At Innoventions you travel down "The Road to Tomorrow." Along the way, stop at each of the interesting exhibits. Some of them teach you about new technologies, while others show you recent inventions for the home or tell you about discoveries in science. New inventions are brought in every three months or so. As Ashley J. says, "The place changes all the time, so you can come again and again." But no matter when you come, you'll get a taste of the future.

Street smarts

Tom Morrow 2.0 is your tour guide at Innoventions. He's an Audio-Animatronic robot who will keep you from getting lost during your trip. There are road signs and street maps, too. Still can't find what you are looking for? Simply ask a cast member to lead you on your way.

HOT TIP
You'll get a better view of the manatees during the day. The light in their tank is dimmed at night so they can sleep.

THE LIVING SEAS

There's something fishy about the animals at The Living Seas. They aren't like any of the other animals in Future World. These critters are all real!

There are more than 2,000 sea creatures living here. It's the world's largest aquarium. There are turtles, dolphins, manatees, and even sharks.

Under the sea

Your sea exploration begins with a short movie. It explains how the earth's oceans were formed. Next, you get in a "hydrolator" (an elevator that goes in water) to go down to see the aquarium. As you get out, ask your parents how deep they think the hydrolator went. Then tell them it moved less than one inch!

Hands-on fun

After a quick ride through the aquarium, you enter an area called Sea Base Alpha. This is your chance to take a closer look at the creatures and to try out the hands-on exhibits.

"The Living Seas is really cool," says Robert. "I thought my ears popped in the hydrolator. It feels like you're going way down to the bottom of the sea."

Brian L. likes the interactive exhibits. "You can put your arms in a diving suit and try to move like you're in the ocean," he says.

Karyn just loves the manatees. "The rest of the exhibits are okay," she says, "but I like to see animals."

THE LAND

The building called The Land looks like a big greenhouse. The attractions inside focus on food and where it comes from. There's a boat ride, a funny show about food, and special guided tours. There's also a movie about the environment. It stars Simba, Timon, and Pumbaa from *The Lion King*.

Study the paintings while you wait in line for Living with the Land. One has bubbles on it that connect to form a Mickey head.

Epcot

Living with the Land

What's the most popular fruit on our planet? The banana! People eat more bananas than any other fruity snack. You'll learn lots more food facts on this boat trip. The boat travels through rooms that look like a rain forest, desert, and prairie. Then it heads to a modern greenhouse area.

A tour guide explains everything your boat floats past. If you're lucky, you'll see some giant vegetables growing here. The greenhouse has produced some of the biggest lemons and eggplants in the world!

In all, The Land grows more than 30 tons of fruit and veggies each year. A lot of it is served to guests in Epcot restaurants.

This boat ride scores high marks with kids. Lindsay says, "The greenhouses are amazing." Anna likes that "it shows us new ways to make the best of our earth."

Hidden Mickey Alert!
Spotlights meet to form this bright Mickey head at the entrance to Food Rocks. Watch carefully though—the effect only lasts a few seconds!

Behind The Seeds Tour

Kids (and parents) who are interested in the environment can sign up for this one-hour guided tour of the growing areas at The Land. It costs $6 for adults, and $4 for kids ages 3 through 9. You'll need reservations. Make them at the front of the Green Thumb Emporium shop.

Food Rocks

Here's a different kind of rock concert with a lesson about good nutrition. These are performers you won't see on any other stage. They are popular musicians who have been turned into familiar foods. They perform old songs with funny new words.

Follow your nose

In the pre-show area, look at the fun food facts painted on the walls. Open one of the "smell boxes" and get a strong whiff of chocolate, garlic, coffee, bacon, orange, or fish. Even the carpet is entertaining, with its pattern of forks, knives, and spoons.

Eat right—or else!

Kids enjoy this show, but it's best for a younger audience. David G. says, "This is a fun way for little kids to learn about nutrition." Jennifer B. adds, "The music makes the subject more entertaining." Dawna thinks the show "makes you feel guilty for eating food that's not good for you."

Most of the kids like the names of the performers and the songs they sing. But some songs are a little old, and sometimes it's hard to make out the lyrics. "It's probably more appealing to adults who know the music," Grace says. "But I think it's a great idea."

Epcot

Hidden Mickey Alert!
Look up in the cloud under the blue balloon at The Land pavilion's center.

The Circle of Life

Simba, Timon, and Pumbaa are together again. This time they're in a movie about the importance of protecting the earth's environment. The film is a mix of animation and live action. It shows some of the problems we face—and how we can fix them.

Timber!

The movie's opening scene shows animals just like those in *The Lion King* (but these animals are real). Next you see Simba near a watering hole. All of a sudden he hears "Timber!" and is drenched by the splash of a tree falling into water. Timon and Pumbaa are clearing the grassland to build a resort (The Hakuna Matata Lakeside Village).

Simba tells a story

Simba remembers what his father taught him about caring for the land. He tells his friends a story about how humans sometimes forget that everything is connected in the great Circle of Life.

Brian F. gets the message of this film. "It means to recycle, don't pollute, and don't litter," he explains. "I like the pictures they took of the fish, birds, alligators, penguins, and bears. And the cartoons are funny."

For Emma, "this movie is a nice reminder about what happens when we forget about the Circle of Life." Ashley J. says, "It really makes you want to change everything. I'm going to recycle more!"

IMAGINATION!

This pavilion is like a workout for your mind—all of the attractions put your imagination to work! There is an interesting and fun ride that tests your imagination, a hands-on activity center, and a wacky 3-D movie called Honey, I Shrunk the Audience. Outside, the jumping waters of the Leap Frog Fountains are sure to keep you guessing. There are a lot of other ways to have fun here, too. Just use your imagination!

HOT TIP

On a hot day, cool off by trying to catch the streams of water that jump from fountain to fountain at the entertaining Leap Frog Fountains.

Journey Into Your Imagination

Think how different the world would be without any imagination in it. There would be no stories to tell, no pictures to draw, and no inventions to make things easier. One thing is for sure—Walt Disney World certainly wouldn't exist! Imagination is so important to Disney that they created a special place in Future World to learn all about it. It's called the Imagination Institute. Here you can go on a trip as far as your mind will take you.

Testing, testing, 1-2-3

The Imagination Institute is having an open house. That means everyone is invited to see and learn about all of its secret projects. As a special guest, you will even be able to test out their latest hi-tech invention—The Imagination Scanner.

It's all in your head

The new Imagination Scanner promises to make you think and look at things in a whole new way.

There are some special effects during the ride that make the tests even more interesting. At one point, it seems like gravity is shut off and your car is moving across the ceiling. Later, a butterfly seems to magically appear on a swing.

Will the Imagination Scanner be a success? That's up to you. If you want the experiments to work, just concentrate, and put *your* imagination to the test.

HoT TiP

Are you a Figment fan? He's not the star of a ride anymore, but you can still spot him on Journey Into Your Imagination. So be on the lookout!

Image Works: Kodak "What If" Labs

Once you get inside Image Works, it may be hard to leave. Kids love it because it's full of hands-on (and feet-on) activities. And now it's even better because there are lots of new things to see and do.

Kids agree that one of their favorite stops is Stepping Tones, where you can step on colored lights to trigger different sounds and reactions. Another popular activity is the Electronic

Philharmonic. There you can conduct an orchestra just by raising and lowering your hands. And there's so much more!

Leah says, "There's a machine that takes your picture and turns it into a flower, animal, or cartoon." Nicholas adds, "You can e-mail the photo to a friend. I was a lizard!" With all there is to do at Image Works, Adam P. has this tip: "Plan to spend at least an hour there!"

Toon Twister

These Disney characters must have gone on too many wild rides. Their heads are spinning! See if you can identify them without getting dizzy yourself.

Character: _____

Character: _____

Character: _____

Character: _____

Character: _____

Character: _____

Honey, I Shrunk the Audience

Remember the kids from *Honey, I Shrunk the Kids*? This 3-D movie gives you an idea of how they felt. That's because this time, you're the one who gets shrunk, along with the rest of the audience. Even the theater seems to shrink.

You get spooked by a thousand 3-D mice, a lion, and one very big and scary snake. Then one of the kids from the movie picks up the theater and carries it around. Somehow you're brought back to real size, but only after some unusual adventures.

Very special effects

As Brian F. tells it: "First the professor shrinks himself. Then he accidentally hits the laser and shrinks us! The people on the screen are really big." Emma adds, "It makes you feel really small."

Ashley J. also finds the effects believable. "I even put my feet up!" she says.

Some scary moments

"I don't think this is a good show for young kids," says Adam P. "They could get scared by the snake and all the mice."

Nicholas also warns, "The show has lots of loud noises." For Jennifer S. the show isn't too scary. "Everything looks like it's jumping right out at you. It's full of surprises." Tate adds, "There's a neat twist at the end." But we won't tell you what it is. As Emma puts it, "I don't want to give any more away. It's nice having a surprise."

Hot Tip
If your hair is long, put it in a ponytail before riding Test Track, or it might get all tangled up.

Hidden Mickey Alert!
This Hidden Mickey is a sweet one! In Area 2B, look for a candy dispenser that's in the shape of that famous mouse.

READER TIP
"If they ask for single riders at Test Track, volunteer! You have to split up from your family on the ride, but you'll bypass the whole line!"

Justin (age 12)
Palatine Bridge, NY

TEST TRACK

What is it like to be a crash test dummy? Find out in this thrilling ride—and learn what new cars go through to be safe for riders.

Where are the brakes?

Test Track is one of Walt Disney World's fastest rides, and Epcot's only thrill ride. The sporty test cars travel on a track that's almost a mile long. Your car has no steering wheel or brake pedals for you to control, but its sound and video equipment lets you know what's being tested. You zip around curves, zoom down a street, and bounce on bumpy roads. At one point, you nearly crash into a truck!

A crash course in car safety

Kids think this ride is a fun way to learn more about cars.

Danielle T. says, "The banks on the curves are incredible. They look really steep. Only ride if you can handle it." Adam P. agrees. "People with motion sickness shouldn't go on this," he says. Leah adds, "The car jerked around a lot at first, but then it started going smooth and fast. That was the coolest part."

Don't worry—it's safer than it looks. Disney workers tested all the cars first. After all, that's what test driving is all about. You must be at least 40 inches tall to try it.

ROUGH
Attraction Reaction

LOUD
Attraction Reaction

SCARY
Attraction Reaction

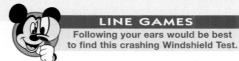

LINE GAMES
Following your ears would be best to find this crashing Windshield Test.

Hidden Mickey Alert!
Look in the mural above Body Wars for a Mickey.
Donald and Goofy are hidden there, too!

WONDERS OF LIFE

You know what you look like on the outside. Now find out what you look like on the inside. This pavilion is all about the human body. It's easy to spend a couple of hours here, so come early to beat the crowds.

HOT TIP
If the sight of blood makes you woozy, don't ride Body Wars.

Epcot

Body Wars

Every time you get a cut, it's white blood cells to the rescue. They destroy infections and help you heal. In this attraction, white blood cells mistake a scientist for an infection. She was shrunk for a special mission inside a body—to remove a nasty splinter. Now the white blood cells are after her!

Your mission is to rescue her before it's too late.

This bumpy ride through a human body takes place in a room called a simulator. Together, the simulator and a movie make you feel like you're inside another person.

You must be at least 40 inches tall to ride.

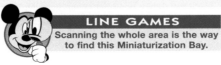

LINE GAMES
Scanning the whole area is the way to find this Miniaturization Bay.

Cranium Command

Imagine that you're a pilot. But instead of flying an airplane, you pilot the brain of a 12-year-old boy. That's what happens to Buzzy during this attraction, and you get to go along for the ride.

Buzzy and the brain

During the pre-show, you stand and watch a funny cartoon that explains how Buzzy gets his job. Then you go into a theater—and inside the brain with Buzzy. You watch as he tries to get all the different parts of the brain to work together.

Kids identify with Bobby

The brain in Cranium Command belongs to a boy named Bobby. (The cranium is the part of your skull where your brain is.) It's Buzzy's job to pilot Bobby through a day at school. "I can relate to the things that happen to the boy in the story," says Tate. Can you?

Epcot

Who am I?

- Most of my friends are toys
- I live in a great big forest
- Honey always tempts my tummy!

Answer: Winnie the Pooh

Fitness Fairgrounds

The lobby of the pavilion has so many hands-on activities, the kids think you can spend at least an hour here.

Wonder Cycles are bikes that let you watch a film while riding. The faster you pedal, the faster the action in the film goes!

In the Coach's Corner, a computer checks your tennis, baseball, and golf swings and gives you tips for a better game. In the Sensory Funhouse, the kids enjoy trying to guess what certain objects are without being able to see them. Justin says, "You can touch everything. It's so much fun."

Who am I?

- My father is the king
- I like to collect things
- I'm sick of swimming!

Answer: Ariel

The Making of Me

Where do babies come from? That question and many more are answered in the film *The Making of Me*. The movie is shown in a theater in the middle of the Wonders of Life pavilion. It lasts 14 minutes. It's a good show to watch with your parents.

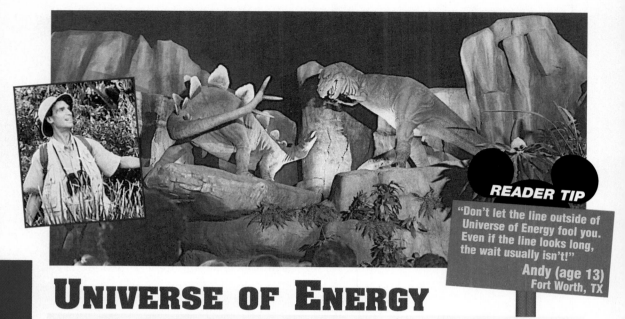

UNIVERSE OF ENERGY

Discover where energy comes from on this trip through prehistoric times, complete with dinosaurs. The ride is called Ellen's Energy Adventure. It's inside the Universe of Energy pavilion.

Ellen's energy nightmare

The attraction starts with a movie about a woman named Ellen. She is asleep and having a weird dream. She's a contestant on a TV game show—and all of the questions are about energy. Ellen doesn't know much about energy, so she really stinks at the game.

Then Bill Nye, the Science Guy, decides to teach her all about energy. To do it, he takes her (and you) on a trip back in time.

Visit the dinosaurs

First you go into a theater to see another movie. Then the ride part begins. Bill Nye takes you and Ellen to a prehistoric world. You travel through fog and past several types of dinosaurs. Some of them are huge. And they all look real.

At the end of the ride, Ellen gets another chance to play on the TV game show. How does she do this time? That's something you'll have to see for yourself!

Three cheers for energy!

The kids who worked on this book loved Ellen's Energy Adventure. Nicholas likes what the ride teaches you about. "It's really interesting," he says. "It's a fun way to learn all about where energy comes from."

If you like dinosaurs, you'll enjoy the ride, too. Adam P. says, "The dinosaurs look so real. They even spit on you." Szasha agrees, "The dinosaur part is my favorite. And Ellen is funny," she adds.

LOUD
Attraction Reaction

DARK
Attraction Reaction

World Showcase

Anyone can be a world traveler at World Showcase. You can learn about other countries, experience different cultures, and meet people from all over the world. Most of the people who work in each pavilion really come from the country they represent. And they're all happy to talk to you.

The pavilions were built around a lake called World Showcase Lagoon. If you make the trip all the way around the lake, you will walk more than one mile!

Hidden Mickey Alert!

The iron grates that the trees in World Showcase grow out of could probably tell a mouse tale or two! They're covered with Hidden Mickeys!

READER TIP

"If you want to learn more about any of the pavilions in Epcot, stop at Guest Relations. They have lots of interesting fact sheets."

Benjamin (age 11)
Geneseo, NY

Epcot

CANADA

If you look at a map of North America, Canada is at the top, just above the United States. It's a beautiful country. The Canada pavilion at Epcot is very pretty, too. There's a rocky mountain, a stream, gardens, and a totem pole.

The highlight is a movie called *O Canada!* The scenes completely surround you. Since you stand during the movie, it's easy to turn around and see everything.

What do the kids who worked on this book think about the movie? David B. explains, "It makes you feel like you're moving."

Ashley P. likes "the music and all the information the movie gives you about Canada."

Karyn says, "All the mountains and sledding scenes are beautiful." Nita agrees. "The movie is pretty," she says. "But I don't like standing up. They need seats in that theater!"

UNITED KINGDOM

From London to the English countryside, this pavilion gives a varied view of the United Kingdom. Some details to look for include the smoke stains painted on the chimneys to make them appear old, and the grassy roofs that are really made of plastic broom bristles. And Tate points out, "There are pretty gardens here."

Lindsay likes "looking at the different stores from the outside."

A group of comedians often performs along World Showcase Promenade near this pavilion. Sometimes, a band plays famous old songs in the garden.

Topiary Trees

There's something unusual about some of the trees growing at Walt Disney World—they're shaped like animals! Some even look like Disney characters. These special plants are called **topiaries** (pronounced:

TOE-pea-air-ees). They're carefully groomed each day by Disney gardeners to keep their exact form. You can spot an Alice topiary by the Mad Tea Party in the Magic Kingdom and a Mary Poppins tree in Epcot's United Kingdom. Walt Disney World has more than 200 topiaries in all. How many can you find?

FRANCE

The Eiffel Tower is probably the best-known landmark at the France pavilion. (The real one is in Paris, France.) The buildings here look just like those in a real French town. Many of the workers here come from France. They speak English with a French accent. Surprise them by saying *bonjour* (pronounced: *bohn-zhoor*). It means "good day" in French.

The main attraction—besides the treats at the bakery—is *Impressions de France* (Impressions of France). It's a movie that takes you from one end of France to the other. It's shown on a big screen, and you get to sit down and take in the sights.

International Mouse

Mickey Mouse is famous all over the world. But not everyone knows the movie-star mouse by that name. In Italy he's called Topolino. In Greece he's known as Miky Maoye. Norwegians call him Mikke Mus. In Sweden he goes by Musse Pigg. And in China he's Mi Lao Shu. That's a lot of names for one mouse to remember!

READER TIP

"If you buy a World Showcase passport you can have it stamped in each country!"
Lyndsey (age 10)
Calgary, Alberta, Canada

MOROCCO

The country of Morocco is famous for its mosaics—artwork and patterns that are made up of many tiles. That's why there is beautiful tile work on the walls of this pavilion. Moroccan artists made sure the mosaics here were done right.

The buildings are copies of monuments in Moroccan cities, including Fez and Marrakesh. There are lots of shops selling things you would find in Morocco. You can buy baskets, brass, jewelry, or a fez (a type of hat) and other Moroccan clothing.

The Marrakesh restaurant has a belly dancer who entertains in the courtyard, too.

Salam alekoum (pronounced: *sah-LAHM wah-LAY-koom*) means "hello" in Morocco.

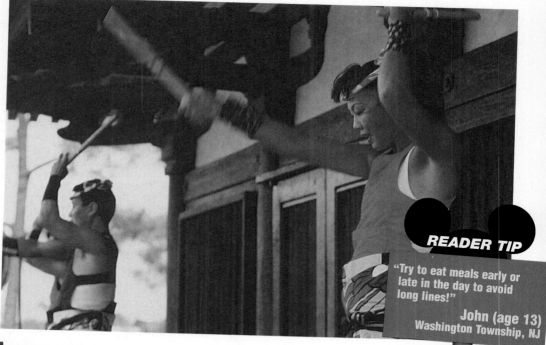

READER TIP

"Try to eat meals early or late in the day to avoid long lines!"

John (age 13)
Washington Township, NJ

Epcot

JAPAN

The giant temple out front, called a pagoda, makes the Japanese pavilion easy to spot. It's modeled after a famous pagoda in the city of Nara, Japan.

Be sure to notice all of the evergreen trees. In Japan, they are symbols of eternal life. Some of the trees found in a traditional Japanese garden will not survive in Florida. So similar trees were used instead.

Japanese drummers often perform outside the pavilion. The huge department store has lots of souvenirs from Japan.

Want to say "good morning" in Japanese? Just say *ohayo gozaimasu* (pronounced: *oh-hi-yoh goh-zy-ee-mahs*).

Just for Kids!

World Showcase has something special for younger kids: Kidcot Fun Stops. There's one in each country. Here you can color and make crafts, and learn how kids have fun in different countries all over the world.

THE AMERICAN ADVENTURE

This pavilion is the centerpiece of World Showcase. It's about the United States of America. That's why it's called The American Adventure.

The American Adventure show takes place inside Independence Hall (the real Independence Hall is in Philadelphia, Pennsylvania). The show celebrates the American spirit from the earliest days right up to the present.

Benjamin Franklin and Mark Twain host the show. They look so real, you may forget that they are mechanical. Ben Franklin even walks up stairs!

The American Adventure honors many heroes from history: the Pilgrims, Alexander Graham Bell, Jackie Robinson, Susan B. Anthony, Walt Disney, and more. Historic events are shown on movie screens.

Anna thinks this show is "a perfect way to learn about our heritage. The best part is the movie that reviews many famous Americans."

Hidden Mickey Alert!

Let your eyes follow the fireworks that burst from behind the Statue of Liberty. One of them leaves a Mickey-shaped puff of smoke.

ITALY

Venice is an Italian city known for waterways called canals. There are no canals at Epcot's Italy, but the pavilion does look a lot like the city. The tower is a smaller version of the Campanile, a famous building in Venice. Notice the gondolas tied to the dock in the lagoon. They are a type of boat used for traveling in the canals of Venice.

Tasty Italian goodies are for sale in the candy shop. The restaurant here is called Alfredo's. Inside, you can watch fresh pasta being made.

Say *buon giorno* (pronounced: *boo-on JOR-no*). It means "good day" in Italian.

Where in the World?

Epcot's World Showcase is bursting with unusual sights and objects. Everything listed below can be found somewhere in its pavilions—and somewhere in this puzzle! (The words are written forward, backward, diagonally, and up and down.) First use a pencil to circle the words in the grid below. Then try to spot these items when you travel through World Showcase.

BELLY DANCER
BONSAI
CHOPSTICKS
CUCKOO CLOCK
EIFFEL TOWER
FEZ
GONDOLA
KIMONO
MARACAS
MARK TWAIN
MOSAICS
PAGODA
PYRAMID
TOTEM POLE
TROLL

```
C E A S M D A T W A I M
R I L D G S G O N F M F
E F C H O P S T I C K S
C F E L N G E E A I I D
N E S Z D L A M W A M I
A L A O O O L P T S O M
D T C O L C L O K N N A
Y O A L A H O L R O O R
L W R L O Y R E A B L Y
L E A G O B T T M S C P
E R M S C I A S O M C K
B C U C K O O C L O C K
```

Hidden Mickey Alert!
You'll find a Mickey in the grass
in Germany's miniature village.

GERMANY

There isn't a village in Germany quite like the one at Epcot. It's a combination of cities and small towns from all around the country. Try to stop by on the hour so you can see the special cuckoo clock and hear it chime.

Danielle G. says, "The buildings in Germany look authentic. In the center is a beautiful statue on top of a waterfall. I also like the cobblestone pavement." Tate suggests you "try the soft pretzels sold here. There's not much else to do, but it's cool to see how some buildings look in Germany."

In German, "good day" is *guten Tag* (say: *GOOT-en tahkh*).

Who am I?

- I live in a tree
- I'm nuts for nuts
- People sometimes think I'm Chip

Answer: Dale

Epcot

CHINA

Disney's version of the Temple of Heaven is at the center of this pavilion. It's a landmark in the Chinese city of Beijing. Inside, there is a Circle-Vision 360 movie called *Wonders of China: Land of Beauty, Land of Time.* (There are no seats in the theater.)

Before going in to see the movie, take a look at the waiting area. It's decorated in red and gold. These colors mean good luck in China.

The movie is beautiful, but it's a little long. It's more popular with adults than kids.

Karyn prefers the waiting area. "I think the movie is boring. But the exhibit is cool," she says.

To say "hello" in Chinese, say *ni hao* (pronounced: *nee HOW*).

READER TIP

"Sit in the back of the boat on Maelstrom for the best view."
Sam (age 15)
San Diego, CA

Epcot

NORWAY

You will discover the history and culture of Norway at this pavilion. (Don't worry about the angry troll. He's harmless.)

The main building is a castle. It was based on an ancient fortress in the capital city of Oslo. Inside, there is a ride called Maelstrom. It's about Norway's history.

He has three heads!

The ride begins in a Viking village. (Vikings were explorers who lived about 1,000 years ago. Many came from Norway.) Next you travel to a forest, where a three-headed troll curses your boat and makes it go

backward! After the boat trip, there is a short movie about Norway.

Short but sweet

How do kids feel about Maelstrom? Dawna says, "I like how we sit in a boat like the ones from Norway." David B. wishes the ride were longer. "I still think it's the best thing in World Showcase, even though it's so short."

Saying "hello" is easy here. It's *god dag* (say: *goo DAHG*).

DARK
Attraction Reaction

HoT TiP
Go to Maelstrom late in the day, when the line is shorter.

- I want to marry a beauty
- My muscles are the biggest around
- Spitting is my specialty

Answer: Gaston

HoT TiP

Don't miss the special entertainment in each of the countries!

Hidden Mickey Alert!
The volcano at the beginning of the boat ride is about to erupt! Watch the swirling smoke carefully and you might spot that famous mouse.

MEXICO

The pyramid-shaped building at the Mexico pavilion is home to El Río del Tiempo: The River of Time. This is a slow boat trip through scenes of Mexican life and history.

Film clips show cliff divers in Acapulco, speed boats in Manzanillo, and beautiful sea creatures in Isla Mujeres. You see many colorful displays showing Mexican traditions. At the end of the boat ride, you can visit several shops with Mexican crafts, sombreros, and colorful blankets.

Brad thinks "the boat ride is fun. There are so many things to look at." Dawna likes "the paintings, because I think Mexican art is really neat." David G. thinks the ride "is a nice way to learn Mexico's history."

"Hello" here is *hola* (say: *OH-lah*).

LINE GAMES
Look for an object that has a wick to find this pointy candlestick.

Entertainment

Epcot is known for its great entertainment. There are lots of shows and special performances every day of the year. For more information, check a park guidemap.

ILLUMINATIONS: REFLECTIONS OF EARTH

An amazing fireworks show takes place each night on and around World Showcase Lagoon. It tells a story of earth's creation. You can get a good view of it from anywhere around the lagoon.

JAMMITORS

One of the loudest and wildest shows is inside Future World, where musicians bang out rhythms on trash cans and, sometimes, on each other. Szasha says, "They're fun and funny."

TAPESTRY OF NATIONS

Join in the fun during this festive parade at World Showcase. The action happens all around you. Fancy puppets and performers wearing unusual costumes and masks dance, sing, and make music with you.

WORLD SHOWCASE PERFORMERS

There is some form of entertainment at each of the pavilions in World Showcase. A couple of the highlights include the Statues in France (they're alive!) and the British Invasion in the United Kingdom. France's Statues are actually people dressed like statues. They look like they are made of stone, but then they surprise you by moving! The British Invasion is a funky band that sounds like The Beatles.

Where to find
CHARACTERS
at EPCOT

Disney characters often appear beside the **Mouse Gear** shop. Sport Goofy can sometimes be spotted at the **Wonders of Life** pavilion.

In World Showcase, you can meet Mickey and his friends at **The American Adventure**. You might find Belle and the Beast near **France**, Jasmine and Aladdin in **Morocco**, and Snow White in **Germany**. But the best spot for character sightings is the **United Kingdom**. Alice, Peter Pan, Mary Poppins, and Winnie the Pooh can sometimes be seen here during the day. Check a park guidemap or ask a cast member who is appearing. And don't forget to ask the characters to sign the autograph section of this book!

EPCOT TIPS

Start your day early at Test Track. Then go to the Wonders of Life pavilion to ride Body Wars and see Cranium Command. If there's time before lunch, see all of the attractions in the Imagination! pavilion.

Remember: World Showcase doesn't open until 11 A.M.

Need a refreshing splash? Visit Cool Wash by Test Track, the squirting sidewalk that leads to World Showcase, or the fountain by Wonders of Life.

Check the electronic Tip Board in Innoventions Plaza. It lets you know how long the wait is for many attractions.

There is a special garbage can in the Electric Umbrella restaurant and a special drinking fountain near The Land pavilion. Why are they special? They talk!

Innoventions is very big and can be tiring. Visit this pavilion early in the day or after a meal, when you are rested and full of energy.

Bring pins with you so you'll have something to trade with other guests at the pin trading booth in Future World. (Get a parent's permission before you trade anything.)

Try not to squeeze the movies at Canada, France, and China all into one day.

Take time to talk to the people who work in World Showcase. Most of them come from the country of the pavilion they represent, and they have many interesting stories to tell.

It might be difficult to walk around World Showcase during the IllumiNations show.

Attraction Ratings

COOL
(Check It Out)

- Food Rocks
- China
- Italy
- United Kingdom
- Mexico
- Germany
- Japan

REALLY COOL
(Don't Miss)

- The Living Seas
- The Circle of Life
- The American Adventure
- Journey Into Your Imagination
- Innoventions
- Mexico boat ride
- France
- Canada
- Morocco
- Fitness Fairgrounds

THE COOLEST
(See at Least Twice)

- Test Track
- Body Wars
- Cranium Command
- Spaceship Earth
- Universe of Energy
- Honey, I Shrunk the Audience
- Norway
- Living with the Land
- Image Works: Kodak "What If" Labs

Epcot

Your favorite Epcot attractions

Disney-MGM Studios

The Disney-MGM Studios lets you see some of the magic of making movies and TV shows. There are attractions that show how animation is done, how sound effects are made, how stunts are performed, and lots more.

The park looks a little like Hollywood did back in the 1940s. Hollywood is the California city where movie-making got its big start. The Disney-MGM Studios got its big start in 1989. Since then lots of famous movies and TV shows have been made there. A crew might even be filming something when you are visiting.

One of the best things about this park is that you can be a part of some attractions. It's fun to be right in the middle of the action, so be sure to volunteer. You will also get to meet a ton of characters, including the stars of some of Disney's recent animated hits—so remember to bring a pen for their autographs.

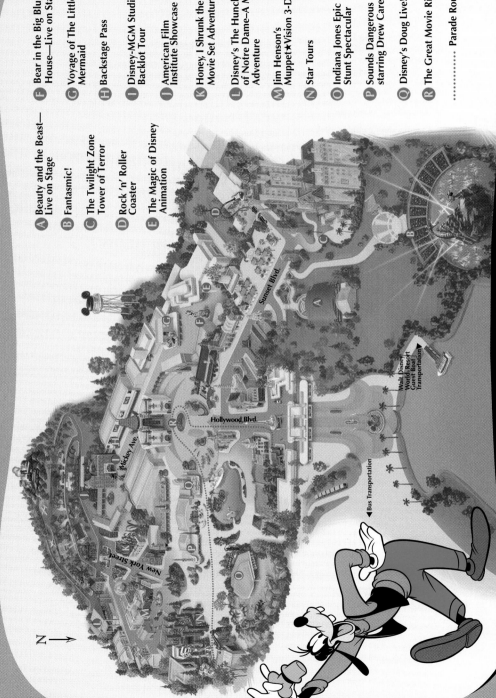

A Beauty and the Beast—Live on Stage

B Fantasmic!

C The Twilight Zone Tower of Terror

D Rock 'n' Roller Coaster

E The Magic of Disney Animation

F Bear in the Big Blue House—Live on Stage

G Voyage of The Little Mermaid

H Backstage Pass

I Disney-MGM Studios Backlot Tour

J American Film Institute Showcase

K Honey, I Shrunk the Kids Movie Set Adventure

L Disney's The Hunchback of Notre Dame–A Musical Adventure

M Jim Henson's Muppet★Vision 3-D

N Star Tours

O Indiana Jones Epic Stunt Spectacular

P Sounds Dangerous starring Drew Carey

Q Disney's Doug Live!

R The Great Movie Ride

········· Parade Route

Sunset Blvd.

Mickey Ave.

Hollywood Blvd.

New York Street

Walt Disney World Resort Guest Boat Transportation▶

▶Bus Transportation

N →

Use this map to explore the Disney-MGM Studios theme park.

The Twilight Zone Tower of Terror

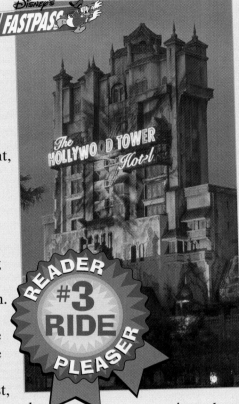

At 199 feet, Tower of Terror is the tallest attraction at Walt Disney World. For some people, it's also the scariest.

Legend says that one Halloween night, lightning hit The Hollywood Tower Hotel. A whole section of the hotel disappeared! So did an elevator carrying five people. No one ever saw them again.

Now the hotel is haunted. If you dare to enter it, you are in for a few surprises. First, you walk through the dusty hotel lobby. Then you enter a tiny room, where Rod Serling appears on TV. (He was the star of a sometimes scary show called *The Twilight Zone*.) Once Rod tells the story of The Hollywood Tower Hotel, get

ready—you are on your way to the Twilight Zone.

Going down!

After waiting in the boiler room for a little while, you are given a seat in a big elevator. The elevator ride takes you on a short tour of the hotel, where you see many special effects. But the highlight comes when the elevator cables snap. Whooosh! You plunge eight stories! Next the elevator shoots up to the hotel's 13th floor. It teeters for a moment and then . . . it drops again and again at blazing speed!

A thrilling experience

People who love thrills think this is a great ride. David G. says, "Get ready because you plunge more than three times. Tower of Terror really lives up to its motto: Fear every drop!"

You must be at least 40 inches tall to ride—and very brave!

Hidden Mickey Alert!

Notice the brass lamp on the podium before you enter the library. The base looks just like Mickey!

LINE GAMES

In board games, you don't have to dabble to find this dusty game of Scrabble.

HoT TiP

Each car's radio plays a different Aerosmith song. Ride more than once to catch a new tune!

Hidden Mickey Alert!

Aerosmith's recording studio is the home of this Hidden Mickey! Look for his shape formed by the electrical cords hanging on the wall.

ROUGH
Attraction Reaction

DARK
Attraction Reaction

SCARY
Attraction Reaction

LOUD
Attraction Reaction

Rock 'n' Roller Coaster starring Aerosmith

This ride really rocks! It travels at top speed and flips you upside down three times. It also has a rock 'n' roll sound track that will have you dancing in your seat.

Rock 'n' Roller Coaster goes really fast—it takes you from zero to 60 miles per hour in the first three seconds of the ride! You need the speed because you're on your way to a party at an Aerosmith concert—and you're running late.

Disney's **FASTPASS**

The ride takes place in a limousine on a roller coaster track. The track looks like a road in California. (You travel on the road to get to the concert.) The limousine's radio is tuned to the concert. You can hear the band is about to begin, but you're not moving yet. Then, just as the concert starts, the light turns green and you're on your way. Hang on!

You must be at least 48 inches tall to ride Rock 'n' Roller Coaster.

LINE GAMES

Search the glass case along the way to find this DISC-O-KID display.

Hidden Mickey Alert!

You might be standing on the biggest Hidden Mickey in this theme park and not even know it. See if you can find it on the map on page 89.

HoT TiP

If you get to this show early, a singing quartet may entertain you while you wait.

Beauty and the Beast Live on Stage

It's hard to keep quiet during this stage show—it makes you want to clap and sing along. The music comes straight from the Disney film *Beauty and the Beast*.

The story is the same, but the order of the songs is different. (A few songs are left out, too.)

Be their guest

The show starts with "Be Our Guest." It's a colorful musical number—just like in the movie. Then the show goes back to the beginning, where Belle is dreaming of faraway places. Soon, she is a prisoner in the Beast's castle. Lumière, Cogsworth, Mrs. Potts, and the rest of the gang are there to help. In the end, the spell is broken. The Beast becomes human again!

A real kid pleaser

Taran says, "If you love the movie, you'll like this show."

"I love when the white doves fly out at the end," says Nita. "I also love the costumes and the music." Karyn enjoys this show, too. "There are so many great details, like the dancing dishes and spoons," she says.

The show is performed several times each day. Read a park guidemap for exact times. (You can get a free map at any shop in the Disney-MGM Studios. Just ask!)

Hot Tip

The sidewalk by The Great Movie Ride is covered with handprints and footprints. They belong to famous stars. Put your palms and feet in the prints and compare your prints with theirs.

Hidden Mickey Alert!

Mickey and pals are drawn onto the Well of Souls. Look for them on the wall during the Indiana Jones scene.

LINE GAMES

Look behind, and ahead of course, to find this pretty painted horse.

The Great Movie Ride

How many movies have you seen in your lifetime? Hundreds? Thousands? Well, how many have you actually been in? Probably not too many! This attraction lets you ride through scenes from old movies.

Pay attention!

First, you'll watch short clips from famous films. Pay close attention—these are the scenes that you will visit later on.

As you enter the ride vehicle, take time to look around. The room is set up like a movie set (a stage where movie scenes are filmed). The background looks like the hills of Hollywood. That's the California town where movie-making got its big start.

A trip to Munchkinland

Once the car starts moving, you'll pass through scenes from movies like *Mary Poppins*, *Alien*, and *Fantasia*. One of the best scenes is straight out of the *Wizard of Oz*. It looks just like Munchkinland! (Beware: The Wicked Witch of the West pops in for a visit.)

You may also get caught in a shootout and come close to being slimed by an alien. The ride ends with a movie that shows more clips from great films.

What do kids think about The Great Movie Ride? "It's really cool," says Robert, "but it could have more action in it." Karyn disagrees. "No matter how many times I ride, I still love it."

DARK
Attraction Reaction

SCARY
Attraction Reaction

Hot Tip

The animators don't work on the weekends. If you want to see them, visit during the week.

The Magic of Disney Animation

Anybody can create a cartoon character. All you need is a pencil, some paper, and a little imagination. But how do you get that character to *move*? That's where the animation part comes in.

Learn how it's done

This attraction shows you how *Fantasia 2000*, *Tarzan*, and other movies were made. It also gives you a chance to watch artists at work on one of Disney's upcoming animated films.

In the waiting area, there are drawings on the walls. Later, you'll find out how artists called *animators* bring these kinds of sketches to life.

Spy on the animators

Toward the beginning of the tour, you get to meet a real Disney artist. There's even time for you to ask questions.

Next, you walk through a studio. It's where many animators work. (They are behind glass walls, so you can see them.) Your tour guide will explain the animation process as you watch. That way you'll understand what the animators are doing.

It takes about 35 minutes to see everything. Try to go early in the day, when the animators are busy working. They usually go home at about 5 o'clock.

You Be The Animator

The artist who made this movie cel is seeing spots! You be the animator and help finish the work. First use colored pencils to fill in all the holes. Then use your imagination to color in the background.

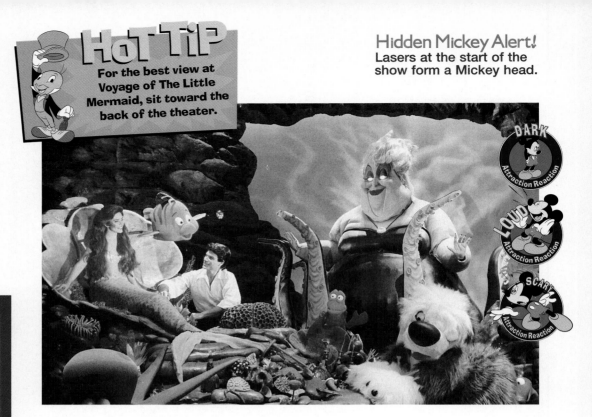

HoT TiP
For the best view at Voyage of The Little Mermaid, sit toward the back of the theater.

Hidden Mickey Alert!
Lasers at the start of the show form a Mickey head.

DARK
Attraction Reaction

LOUD
Attraction Reaction

SCARY
Attraction Reaction

Disney-MGM Studios

Voyage of The Little Mermaid

You don't have to be a fish to have fun underwater — and this show proves it. In it, you go below the ocean's surface with Ariel and her friends from *The Little Mermaid*. They sing and act out the story on stage. Ariel and Eric are played by actors. Flounder, Sebastian, and other creatures are puppets.

Under the sea

There are some great special effects that draw you into the show. A screen of water makes it seem like the theater really is under the sea. Lasers flash, lightning strikes, and mist sprays

DISNEY'S FASTPASS

the audience. Scenes from the movie are shown on a big screen behind the stage.

A winning combination

Dawna thinks "the combination of actors, puppets, movie clips, lasers, bubbles, and water all add up to a great show."

Lindsay agrees. "This is a totally creative show. You feel like you're under the water, especially when you get a little wet with the mist."

Tate thinks they leave out too much of the story. "Even though most people know what happens, it would be better to have more scenes," he says.

Who am I?

- I fall down holes
- Mystery drinks make me shrink
- Today is my un-birthday!

Answer: Alice in Wonderland

Bear in the Big Blue House Live on Stage

Do you know how to do the cha-cha? Well Bear does, and he'll be happy to show you how in this sweet musical stage show. All of Bear's friends are along for the performance, too. So if you're a fan of the Disney Channel's *Bear in the Big Blue House* show, you're sure to have a good time.

Home sweet home

When you walk into the auditorium you'll notice something unusual about it—there are no seats. But don't worry, the carpet is comfy, so sit down and make yourself at home. Soon Bear, Tutter, Pip, Pop, and the rest of the gang will be on stage to sing and dance, and have lots of fun.

Where's Tutter?

Bear's friend Tutter is a little bit shy about dancing in front of everyone. But soon enough he realizes there is nothing to be afraid of and he's ready to show off his moves. Are you in a dancing mood? When the song starts that's your cue to stand up and dance to the music. Little kids seem to have the most fun dancing along with Bear, so if you have younger brothers or sisters be sure to bring them to this show!

Hot Tip

You can sing in the rain under a special umbrella on New York Street.

Disney-MGM Studios

Who am I?

- I have a knack for inventing things
- I think the princess is swell
- I brought the circus to town!

Answer: 게브

READER TIP

"Look for machines in the parks that press a design into a penny. The coins make a great souvenir!"

Kate (age 13)
Shrewsbury, PA

Hot Tip

Ask a cast member or check a guidemap to find out if a TV show or movie is being filmed during your visit.

Backstage Pass

Do you know what you want to be when you grow up? An actor? How about a movie director? In either case, this is the attraction for you. Here you'll get a chance to see how these jobs are done. The tour shows how scenes from movies and television shows like *Home Improvement* were created.

Tricks of the trade

Backstage Pass teaches you lots of movie-making tricks. You'll see how film shot in front of a blue screen can be combined with a different background, to make the action look like it's happening somewhere else.

Lights! Camera! Action!

"I've never been on a tour that took me backstage like that," says Michael. "We got to see actual props from a movie." You might even be able to see a real scene from a movie or a television show being filmed. If a crew is filming when you visit, you can watch the action happen on one of the attraction's soundstages.

98

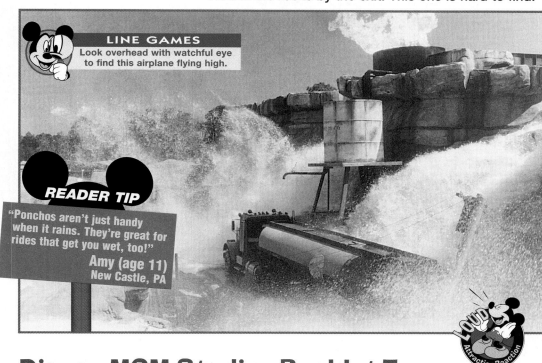

LINE GAMES
Look overhead with watchful eye to find this airplane flying high.

READER TIP
"Ponchos aren't just handy when it rains. They're great for rides that get you wet, too!"
Amy (age 11)
New Castle, PA

LOUD Attraction Reaction

Disney-MGM Studios Backlot Tour

There's a real working studio at this theme park. A tram ride lets you see parts of the backstage areas where movies and TV shows are filmed. You also see how a battle scene at sea is shot.

A grand canyon

The trip includes a stop at Catastrophe Canyon—a special effects area. Here you see a fire and a flash flood. (You may get a little bit wet.) The tram also takes you through the costume department, and past props from famous movies.

"I like Catastrophe Canyon," says Lissy. "It shows that special effects are safer than they look."

Robert agrees. "Catastrophe Canyon is really cool. When the explosions go off, it gets really hot. Then when the water comes down, it gets really cold."

Where's the back door?

Ashley P. enjoys touring the streets and "seeing the houses without the backs. They only film the fronts for the television shows, so that's all they build," she points out.

Nita has seen this attraction before. "I like this tour," she says, "but a lot depends on the guide. If you get a really good guide, the tour is much better."

Honey, I Shrunk the Kids Movie Set Adventure

The backyard from the *Honey, I Shrunk the Kids* movie has been re-created as a big playground. Even grown-ups feel small here. There are 30-foot blades of grass, huge Lego blocks, a giant ant, and more. There are things to climb on, slide down, and explore.

"It looks more like *Honey, I Blew Up the Garden*!" says Taran.

Lissy thinks "the whole place is really neat. Not just the slides and the swings—there's a lot for older kids to notice. Everything looks like it comes straight from the movie."

Most kids enjoy getting wet under the leaky hose. Water squirts from a different spot each time.

"I like the slides and the big net, but I think it's more for younger kids," says Brian L.

Karyn agrees. "I'm the type of person who would just love to take younger kids around and watch them have fun."

Hot Tip

There's a big map at the entrance to Honey, I Shrunk the Kids Movie Set Adventure. Use it!

Who am I?

- I don't get out much
- I used to be a star
- I'm a real stinker

Answer: Stinky Pete

Hidden Mickey Alert!

The Muppets have made some Hidden Mickeys of their own! Look on their building for funny eyes and noses that together form the shape of Mickey heads.

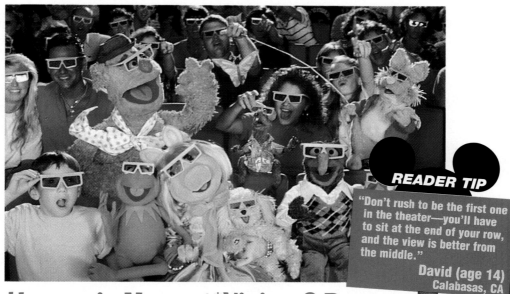

READER TIP

"Don't rush to be the first one in the theater—you'll have to sit at the end of your row, and the view is better from the middle."

David (age 14)
Calabasas, CA

Disney-MGM Studios

Jim Henson's Muppet*Vision 3-D

Don't miss this attraction—it's one of Walt Disney World's best. It begins with a funny pre-show starring Fozzie Bear, Gonzo, Scooter, and Sam Eagle. Then you go into a special theater that looks just like the one from the old *Muppet Show*. Here, you see 3-D movie effects mixed with some other special effects. Sometimes it's hard to tell what's part of the movie and what's real.

Amazing effects

"The characters come right out at you," says Lissy. "It's cool that they have real things happening, so when they throw a pie you think it will be real." Adam W. enjoys the show. "My favorite parts are the squirting water

and when the screen blows up. You feel like you're going to get hit."

Kirsti is a Muppet fan, too. "This is my favorite show and it always will be," she says. Taran thinks "it's awesome. I also love the little 3-D character, Waldo, because he seems like he's talking only to you." (Waldo is a special character that was dreamed up just for this show.)

Look around the theater

Nita says to look at the back of the theater "because a lot happens back there and most people miss it."

Karyn says, "You have to see this movie a few times to get all the jokes and appreciate more of the details, like the two guys sitting in the balcony. They're really funny."

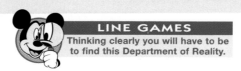

LINE GAMES
Thinking clearly you will have to be to find this Department of Reality.

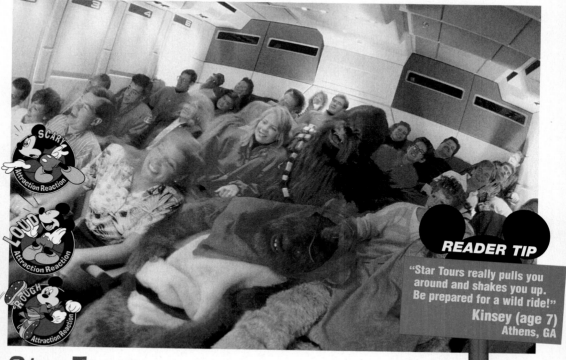

SCARY
Attraction Reaction

LOUD
Attraction Reaction

ROUGH
Attraction Reaction

READER TIP

"Star Tours really pulls you around and shakes you up. Be prepared for a wild ride!"
Kinsey (age 7)
Athens, GA

Disney-MGM Studios

Star Tours

DISNEY'S
FASTPASS

Soar through the galaxy on an out-of-control spaceship and experience the thrills of the movie *Star Wars*. Your pilot is Captain Rex. He's new on the job and can't seem to find his way through all the giant ice crystals and other spaceships.

It feels real

This ride takes place on a flight simulator, the same type used to train astronauts and pilots. The combination of the simulator and the movie makes you feel like you're really rocketing through outer space.

Rex is a rotten pilot

Brad says, "The pilot makes this ride really fun. He keeps going the wrong way." Robert thinks "it's really neat. It's funny when the pilot can't find the brakes."

Danielle G. agrees. "It feels and looks like you're really traveling through space." Dawna adds, "It seems like you're going really fast even though you're not actually going anywhere."

This ride may take a new high-speed trip through space during your visit. You must be at least 40 inches tall to experience Star Tours.

Disney's Doug Live!

Everybody's favorite boy from 21 Jumbo Street comes to life in this entertaining musical show. All of the characters are played by humans—even Porkchop, Doug's trusty pup. But the actors sound and act a lot like the cartoon characters, so they are easy enough to recognize.

HOT TIP

If you volunteer to play Quailkid, be prepared to wear underwear over your pants!

Name that tune

In the beginning of the show, Doug wins a radio contest by identifying a silly song. The prize is two tickets to The Beets concert. He wants to go with Patti, his favorite girl in the whole world. But Roger asks her first.

Quailman to the rescue!

Doug is feeling very bad about himself. But his alter-ego Quailman tells him all he has to do is be himself, and Patti will like him. As it turns out, he's right.

During the concert, some of the action happens right in the audience. David G. advises: "Sit in the front and Doug and Skeeter will sit right by you to watch The Beets. It makes you feel like you're in the show."

Some guests really *are* in the show. Jennifer B. says, "Being Quailkid would make the experience even more special. If you're not picked, ask a parent to volunteer to play a Beet."

Hidden Mickey Alert!

Mickey has always been a star but now he is *in* the stars, too! Look for a giant Mickey constellation in the wall by the pizza counter. Mushrooms, pizza cutters, and pizza slices, are also hidden in this mural.

Toy Story Pizza Planet Arcade

This arcade and restaurant looks a lot like Andy's favorite pizza place from the movie *Toy Story*. It's located near Jim Henson's Muppet*Vision 3-D. If you have trouble finding it, just look for the giant Mr. Potato Head and Rex the dinosaur sitting on top of the building. Inside are lots of "claw" prize machines and video games, plus a fast-food counter with pizza, salad, and juice boxes. Brian F. says, "I like it because it's just like the movie."

Disney's The Hunchback of Notre Dame—A Musical Adventure

You are invited to the Festival of Fools. The celebration is packed with dancers and puppets, all dressed in colorful costumes.

This live show is based on Disney's animated film *The Hunchback of Notre Dame*. If you've seen the movie, you'll know the characters. The storyteller is Clopin, King of the Gypsies. He gets lots of help from his band of gypsy players, who sing, dance, and act out the tale. Quasimodo, Judge Frollo, Esmeralda, and Phoebus also make appearances. And those wacky gargoyles, Victor, Hugo, and Laverne are there to make everybody laugh.

Szasha says, "I think it's a cool play, even though I haven't seen the movie. I like the puppets and live actors. Quasimodo rings the bells by pulling a rope, and they really work." Danielle T. likes "how the actors go into the audience. Their costumes are great."

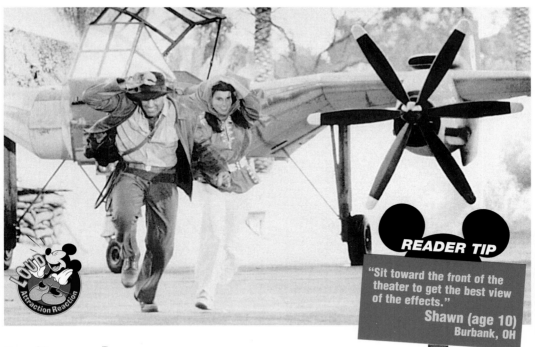

READER TIP

"Sit toward the front of the theater to get the best view of the effects."

Shawn (age 10)
Burbank, OH

Indiana Jones Epic Stunt Spectacular

Fire, explosions, daring escapes, and other special effects are the stars of this attraction. Stunt men and women act out scenes from the movie *Raiders of the Lost Ark* and show how special effects are done. The audience watches from a large theater, and several adults are chosen to perform with the pros. (It's too dangerous for kids.)

Fun for everyone

"I love this show. I think it's great for all ages," says Karyn. One of the best parts of the show is the re-creation of the scene in the movie where the giant ball rolls down and seems to crush Indiana Jones. "I was at the edge of my seat!" says Brian L.

Don't try this at home

Lissy says the music adds to the suspense and "the stunt people are just fantastic." Brian L. views it as pure excitement: "I love how they were falling from the towers, and then they were always okay."

You learn a lot about movie stunts at this show. "They explain everything they do, making it even more fun to watch," says Karyn.

HoT TiP
After the show, visit the area by the exit called Sound Works, for some do-it-yourself sound effects.

Sounds Dangerous starring Drew Carey

You may have seen a 3-D movie before, but have you ever seen a movie with 3-D sound? For this one you have to wear special headphones that make the action sound like it's happening all around you.

Inspector Carey

Drew Carey is the hero of this funny movie. He's supposed to be an actor whose character is an undercover detective. But the detective is not very good at his job. And he's wearing a camera, so the audience can see (and hear) all the mistakes he makes.

Lights out!

Drew sneaks into a warehouse to spy on some jewel smugglers. When he runs into a security guard, he panics—and hides the camera in his mouth (which breaks it, of course).

The next thing you know the theater is dark and you can only hear what's going on through your headphones. The sounds seem so real that the action is easy to follow.

For Jennifer S. this show is a favorite. "It was great! When the lights went off, everything felt so real. You could actually feel people breathe in your ear!" she says.

Mystery Meanie

These six Disney villains are all quite evil, but only one of them is the Mystery Meanie in question. Use the clues below to crack the case.
Bonus: Can you name all six meanies?

MYSTERY MEANIE CLUES

A. I'M NOT SMILING
B. I AM NOT WEARING A HAT
C. I DO NOT HAVE HORNS
D. MY TEETH AREN'T WHITE

Who Am I? _____

Entertainment

Lights! Camera! Action! There's a lot of star-studded entertainment at the Disney-MGM Studios. Most of it has a TV or movie theme. Two of the best shows are described below.

FANTASMIC!

What does Mickey Mouse dream about? You can find out at Fantasmic! It's an amazing show that combines laser lights, Disney characters, movies, music, and a little magic.

Mickey's dreams are fun to watch—but some of them are a little scary. (Disney villains keep turning his dreams into nightmares.) In the end, good wins over evil and Mickey's dreams are happy once more.

Fantasmic! is presented nightly in a theater behind The Twilight Zone Tower of Terror attraction. It's very popular, so be sure to line up at least an hour before the show starts. And, if it isn't summer, bring a jacket or a sweater—it can get chilly!

MULAN PARADE

The star of *Mulan* rides in a parade on Hollywood Boulevard every afternoon. Look for fancy floats, brave soldiers, and giant puppets, plus the Matchmaker, Shang, the villain Shan-Yu on a giant bed of skulls, and Mulan's trusty sidekick, Mushu the dragon.

Where to find
CHARACTERS
at the Disney-MGM Studios

There are lots of places to meet Disney characters at the Studios. One of the best spots is **Mickey Avenue**. Disney characters stop by all day. Go late in the afternoon when there aren't as many people, and you can get a ton of pictures. If you check a park guidemap or ask a cast member, you can find the times that characters are scheduled to appear.

You won't find Mickey on Mickey Avenue. He's in **Animation Courtyard** posing for pictures and signing autographs all day long. Stop by and say hello!

If you want to pose with the characters over breakfast or lunch, have a meal at the **Hollywood & Vine** restaurant. Ask each character to sign the autograph section at the back of this book.

DISNEY-MGM STUDIOS

Arrive at the Disney-MGM Studios before the opening time. The gates usually open about a half hour before the scheduled time.

The character breakfast at the Hollywood & Vine restaurant is a great way to start the day.

There are "chicken exits" at both Tower of Terror and Rock 'n' Roller Coaster, just in case you change your mind at the last minute.

The Tip Boards on Hollywood Boulevard and New York Street tell you which rides have the shortest lines and when the next shows start.

Some stage shows don't open until late morning. Be sure to check your guidemap for exact showtimes.

To get a good spot to see the afternoon parade, line up on Hollywood Boulevard about 30 minutes early.

Mickey Avenue is the best place to meet Disney characters.

The front rows at Fantasmic! get wet. The best seats are in the back at either end of the theater.

See Jim Henson's Muppet*Vision 3-D, Voyage of The Little Mermaid, and Star Tours in the morning before the lines get too long.

Attraction Ratings

COOL
(Check It Out)

- The Great Movie Ride
- Backstage Pass
- Disney's The Hunchback of Notre Dame—A Musical Adventure
- Bear in the Big Blue House Live on Stage

REALLY COOL
(Don't Miss)

- Indiana Jones Epic Stunt Spectacular
- Disney-MGM Studios Backlot Tour
- Honey, I Shrunk the Kids Movie Set Adventure
- Disney's Doug Live!
- Fantasmic!

THE COOLEST
(See at Least Twice)

- Jim Henson's Muppet*Vision 3-D
- Star Tours
- Tower of Terror
- Beauty and the Beast Live on Stage
- The Magic of Disney Animation
- Voyage of The Little Mermaid
- Sounds Dangerous starring Drew Carey
- Rock 'n' Roller Coaster

Your favorite Disney-MGM Studios attractions

Disney's Animal Kingdom

The newest park in Walt Disney World is called Animal Kingdom. It celebrates animals of every kind, from lions, tigers, and zebras to giant turtles whose ancestors lived during the time of the dinosaurs. And they're all real! You may get closer to them than you've ever been before. There are dinosaurs, too. The dinos aren't real, but they sure seem it.

Animal Kingdom is a theme park with many attractions. Just like at the Magic Kingdom, there are different "lands" to visit in Animal Kingdom. The major lands are Safari Village, DinoLand U.S.A., Asia, Africa, and Camp Minnie-Mickey.

You enter the park through The Oasis. It's a big garden with plants and animals. Take some time to look around. Then cross a bridge to Safari Village, admire the giant Tree of Life, and then decide which land to explore first.

ASIA

J Flights of Wonder at Caravan Stage

K Maharajah Jungle Trek

L Kali River Rapids

DINOLAND U.S.A.

M Dinosaur

N The Boneyard playground

O Cretaceous Trail

P Tarzan™ Rocks!

AFRICA

A Kilimanjaro Safaris

B Pangani Forest Exploration Trail

C Wildlife Express to Conservation Station

D Conservation Station

SAFARI VILLAGE

E The Tree of Life

F Safari Village Trails

G It's Tough to be a Bug!

CAMP MINNIE–MICKEY

H Festival of the Lion King

I Pocahontas and Her Forest Friends

ASIA

DINOLAND U.S.A.

THE OASIS

SAFARI VILLAGE

AFRICA

CAMP MINNIE-MICKEY

ENTRANCE PLAZA

N

What's the best way to see Animal Kingdom? Use this map to help you decide!

Safari Village

Safari Village is the island gateway to all the other lands in the park. The Tree of Life stands near the center of Safari Village. If you wander about its roots you'll see all kinds of animals.

Hidden Mickey Alert!
There's a mouse in the moss! Look for clusters of moss near the tiger. They form a Hidden Mickey.

The Tree of Life

This man-made tree is 145 feet tall. From far away it looks like any other tree. But when you get up close, you'll realize that this is not an ordinary tree. It's covered with animals!

Artists have carved 325 animal images into its trunk. In fact, it's called The Tree of Life because it's covered with so many different kinds of animal life.

Jennifer B. says, "It's a must-see. Although I guess it's fairly hard to miss a 14-story-tall tree!" she adds. Grace has a tip: "The best place to get a close look at the animals carved into the tree is while waiting in line for It's Tough to be a Bug!"

It's Tough to be a Bug!

The Tree of Life has a hollow trunk. It's cool, dark, and roomy inside. That makes it a great place to watch a 3-D movie called It's Tough to be a Bug! It's hosted by Flik, the star of *A Bug's Life*.

This movie is about the tiny creatures that outnumber all others on our planet—bugs. In it, animated insects use music and special effects to show how hard their lives are, so that humans won't want to hurt them anymore.

SCARY Attraction Reaction

DARK Attraction Reaction

LOUD Attraction Reaction

Most of the bugs are friendly and funny. But when Flik's enemy Hopper makes an appearance, the show gets a little bit scary.

Kids love this exciting show. As Jennifer B. says, "The effects make it seem so real!" Leah adds, "I really like it when it feels like the bugs are crawling under your seat." David G. has a warning: "Watch out for the stink bug!"

READER TIP

"At It's Tough to be a Bug!, be sure to sit back straight in your chair so you won't miss a thing."

Chelsea (age 12)
Howell, NJ

LINE GAMES

You do not have to feel her sting to find this Beauty who loves to sing.

Disney's Animal Kingdom

Who am I?

- I always wear a badge
- Pull my string to hear me talk
- My favorite place is Andy's room

Answer: Woody

DinoLand U.S.A.

The entrance to this land is marked by a giant dinosaur skeleton. Inside, you will find life-like dinosaurs as well as live animals that have existed since prehistoric times. The main attraction is Dinosaur, but there are lots of other things to see and do. For a hand-clapping good time, swing by Tarzan Rocks! at the Theater in the Wild. In DinoLand you can also dig for bones in an amazing playground, learn about real dinosaurs, or spend some quiet time on a short nature trail.

Cretaceous Trail

For a break from the crowds, take a walk down the Cretaceous Trail. This short path is filled with plants and animals that have been around longer than people have. Their ancestors lived with real dinosaurs! Be on the lookout for crocodiles. You may even hear the rumblings of some pretend dinosaurs. Keep in mind that the trail is changing, and may look different when you visit.

Dinosaur

This thrilling ride takes guests back to the last few minutes of the Cretaceous Period. (That's when the dinosaurs died out.) Kids who have been to Animal Kingdom before will remember the ride by its old name—Countdown to Extinction.

Save the dinosaur

The mission for Dinosaur is to save the last iguanodon. You have to brave a meteor shower and the largest Audio-Animatronic creature Disney has ever made. It's a dinosaur called a carnotaurus, and it may be the ugliest thing you've ever seen. This monster has the face of a toad, horns like a bull, and squirrel-like arms. It looks like it's alive. The nostrils even move as it breathes. And, boy, can it run. The carnotaurus runs for about 30 feet. Be careful! This hungry monster is not just after the iguanodon—it wants to eat *you*, too.

An exciting (and scary) ride

The kids agree that this is a very exciting ride, but one that might not be for everyone. "This is one of the most thrilling rides," says David G., "but it might be way too scary for some kids." Grace feels the same way. "It's bumpy and the dinosaurs seem so real. That's what makes it so much fun," she adds. Jennifer B. loves the scary factor. "This is one of the best rides I've ever been on!" she says. (Kids who don't like scary rides can find some quieter dino encounters on the Cretaceous Trail.)

You must be at least 40 inches tall to ride.

READER TIP

"Dinosaur is very loud and dark, and it really jerks and pulls you around. Some young kids won't like it at all!"

Julia (age 11)
Prairieville, LA

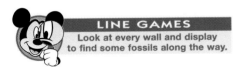

LINE GAMES
Look at every wall and display to find some fossils along the way.

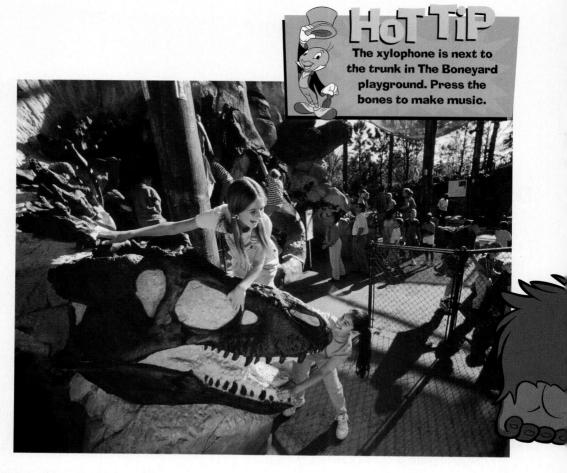

The Boneyard

Are you ready to dive into the biggest sandbox you've ever seen? It's here and it's filled with bones! You can uncover the bones of a mammoth and find clues about how the animal died.

There are also dinosaur footprints that roar when you jump in them, and a xylophone that's made of dinosaur bones. There's a rope maze for climbing and plenty of slippery slides, too. Be sure to check out the OldenGate Bridge. It's made from a huge dinosaur skeleton.

Kids have a fun time exploring the Boneyard. David G. says, "You really feel like you're an archeologist searching for bones and fossils."

Tarzan™ Rocks!

The stars of this musical show can't stay still. And you won't be able to, either. As soon as it starts you'll be tapping your toes and dancing in your seat to rock versions of songs from the movie *Tarzan*.

Rock and roll show

The band is rocking and the performers are rolling—literally! They're wearing in-line skates instead of shoes. Even on wheels they can dance and jump, and do all sorts of tricks in the air.

Jungle Boogie

Lots of the characters in the show wear in-line skates, but Tarzan doesn't. Actually, he doesn't wear shoes at all—that would make it much harder for him to swing from the vines! Does Jane come along for the ride? Of course! Would *you* pass up an opportunity like that? Jane, Tarzan, and Terk all make an appearance, but the dancers and singers are really the stars of this energetic show.

Loud Attraction Reaction

Africa

Before creating this land, Disney Imagineers spent months on the continent of Africa learning all about the plants and animals there. When they came back, they made an African forest and a grassland in Florida. Then they filled it with hundreds of the same animals they had seen in Africa. Most of the animals in Animal Kingdom came from special parks and zoos around the world. You can see many animals on a safari ride and learn all about them at Conservation Station.

Kilimanjaro Safaris

DISNEY'S FASTPASS

In this wild jungle adventure, you ride in a vehicle that's wide open. There's almost nothing between you and the animals! You may see hippos, lions, giraffes, rhinos, elephants, and more. Some animals may even come up close. But don't worry—the dangerous animals can't get near you.

After a calm sight-seeing tour, the ride takes a different twist. There are poachers hunting for elephants, and the animals need your help. The safari ride ends with a wild chase over muddy roads to catch the bad guys. Eric says, "Chasing the poachers isn't scary. But driving over the broken bridge is!"

Kids love the Kilimanjaro Safaris. It's Grace's favorite ride in Animal Kingdom. "I've never been so close to animals like that before," she says. "Some of them even came right up to our jeep!" Jennifer B. adds.

LINE GAMES
While waiting in line do make it your task to find this African tribal mask.

Pangani Forest Exploration Trail

After you take a ride on the Kilimanjaro Safaris, go for a walk on the Pangani Forest Exploration Trail. This nature trail is filled with many exciting sights. You'll come nose-to-nose with a naked mole rat and look for hippos underwater. Exotic fish and birds live in the African Aviary.

No binoculars necessary

Pick up a bird guide (they should be hanging on a post in the aviary) and see how many different birds you can spot. Afterward, make a stop at the meerkat exhibit. Some people call it the "Timon exhibit" because he's a meerkat. (There are no Pumbaas here, though. Meerkats and warthogs don't get along in real life.)

Greetings, gorillas

At the end of the trail, you see a family of gorillas. They are usually hanging out on the hills or playing. You might even spot a baby gorilla in the group. Szasha says, "Seeing the gorillas up close is amazing."

Who am I?

- I've always been a big wimp
- I like to keep things squeaky clean
- Piranhas! They're my greatest fear!

Answer: Tantor

HoT TiP

Pick up a Fastpass for Kilimanjaro Safaris before you board the Wildlife Express. Then when you return it may be your time for the safari.

Hidden Mickey Alert!

There are Mickeys hiding all over the colorful mural at the entrance to the main building! Look for them in the eyes of the animals and on the wings of the butterflies.

Conservation Station

There's only one way to get to Conservation Station: on a train called the Wildlife Express. You can hop aboard in Africa. During the ride you get a behind-the-scenes look at the buildings where animals from the safari ride are cared for.

Lend a helping hand

The exhibits at Conservation Station teach you what animals need to survive—and what people can do to help. There is an animal hospital, places for baby animals to sleep and get special care, and lots of shows meant to get you excited about conservation. There are even ways to find out about conservation projects near your home.

Talk to the animals

Many exhibits at Conservation Station are interactive. In Song of the Rainforest, you're surrounded by the sounds you might hear in a real rain forest. At the Look-in Lab, you can sometimes watch veterinarians care for baby animals. People can walk among animals like goats and sheep in the Affection Section. Go ahead and pet them, but remember: Feeding is not allowed.

Everybody has a favorite exhibit here. "Really young kids might like to pet the animals, but I like Song of the Rain Forest best," Eric says.

Kids care

The kids feel that Conservation Station is an important part of the park. "I'm glad there's a conservation area so we can learn to save the animals," Danielle T. says. Szasha agrees. "If we don't help them, they could become extinct," she adds.

Creature Connection

Rafiki says that all creatures big and small are connected by the great circle of life. In this puzzle Simba and Flik are connected in another way, too—they're linked by letters. Eighteen names are listed below, but you'll only need twelve of them to complete the puzzle. Can you figure out which characters will do the trick? We've filled in some names and a few of the linking letters to help you on your way.

ABU
ATTA
BALOO
BAMBI
DUMBO
FLOUNDER
FLOWER
FRANCIS
HOUND
MUFASA
NALA
PERDITA
PUMBAA
RAFIKI
SCUTTLE
TANTOR
THUMPER
TIMON

Asia

Asia is the largest continent on earth. It's almost twice as big as North America! The land called Asia in Animal Kingdom is a lot smaller than the real thing, but it gives you an idea of what the Asian continent is like. It has jungles and rain forests and magnificent animals. It's also home to the fastest raging river in Animal Kingdom. If you want to get wet, you can shoot the rapids down the river on a ride called Kali River Rapids. For a calmer experience, make a trip to the Caravan Stage.

Maharajah Jungle Trek

Put on your walking shoes and keep your eyes peeled. This jungle trail is the place to spot strange, scaly animals called Komodo dragons, deer, giant fruit bats (they snack on melon), and lots of tigers. You'll also see many colorful birds along the way and tons of plants and trees. Pick up a map at the beginning of the trail to know what to look for.

You see the bats about halfway through your walk. Their wings are enormous! In some places, there's no glass between you and the bats. But don't worry—they're not interested in humans. Still, the kids agree that the bats can be a little creepy to look at. If you don't like bats, take Grace's advice: "Go when the sun is out. The bats are nocturnal, so they're not very active during the day."

Hidden Mickey Alert!
The mural by the tigers is where this Mickey head is hiding!

Kali River Rapids

This is one of the wettest and wildest rides in Walt Disney World. Don't bother trying to pick a dry seat on the raft, because everyone gets wet! It begins as a peaceful raft trip through a rain forest. But things don't stay calm for very long. The raft bumps along down the river, spinning and turning every time it hits a rock. Along the way you catch a glimpse at how logging (cutting down trees for lumber) can destroy the rain forest. Don't be scared if you see a fire raging out of control—that's just part of the ride. You avoid the burning logs, but will you be safe from the waterfall? We won't tell.

FASTPASS (You might want to bring a towel, just in case!)

Guests must be at least 42 inches tall to ride the rapids.

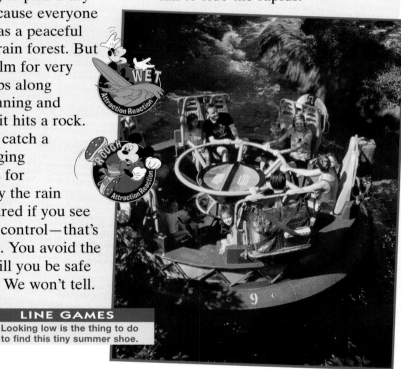

LINE GAMES

Looking low is the thing to do to find this tiny summer shoe.

Flights of Wonder

Live birds are the stars of this show that takes place on the Caravan Stage. They swoop and soar and do amazing tricks.

Sometimes one of the performers is an African Grey parrot named Quasar. He loves to impress the audience. What is his special talent? He's a whiz at math. He can answer all the math questions as fast as a human can. And sometimes even faster!

Camp Minnie-Mickey

Disney characters have their very own vacation spot right here in Animal Kingdom. It's called Camp Minnie-Mickey and it's a great place to meet characters like Mickey, Minnie, Goofy, Pooh, Rafiki, and their friends. To find your favorite characters, just follow the trails through the forest. But save time to see the two shows while you're here.

Pocahontas and Her Forest Friends

Who can save the forest? The wise old tree, Grandmother Willow, knows the answer. But she won't tell. She wants Pocahontas to figure it out for herself.

This show is performed at Grandmother Willow's Grove. It takes you and Pocahontas on a journey through the forest.

Together, you'll meet many different animals: a porcupine, a skunk, a raccoon, a possum, even a snake. And they are all real! During the show, you will learn that every animal has its own special talent. You'll also discover which animal can stop the forest from being destroyed.

Hidden Mickey Alert!
This Hidden Mickey is formed by three stones on a dirt path. Look for it on the mural by the stage.

READER TIP

"Remember to bring a water bottle with you to Animal Kingdom on hot days."

Meg (age 12)
Vero Beach, FL

Disney's Animal Kingdom

Festival of the Lion King

This is one spectacular musical show. Even if you have the movie memorized, you're in for a few surprises. Many of the major characters from the movie are here, but they look a little different. Most of them are played by humans dressed in colorful African costumes.

An action-packed performance

The theater has big stages that look like parade floats. (That's because they were once used in a parade at Disneyland!) On one, Simba sits atop Pride Rock. The wisecracking Pumbaa sits on another. Gymnasts dressed like monkeys use the center stage as a trampoline. They jump and do tricks.

Kids love the festival

"It's a terrific stunt show," David G. says. Grace agrees. "The songs and characters are wonderful," she adds. Jennifer B. thinks "the whole show is great, but the monkeys are the best part!" Eric loves it too, but he warns: "Expect some loud noises and flames that burst up suddenly."

This is a very popular show. Check a park guidemap for times and arrive at least 30 minutes before it starts.

LINE GAMES
Peek at the trees where you think best to find this house for birds to nest.

Entertainment

Don't be surprised if the performers at Animal Kingdom come right up to you—some walk on two legs, while others walk on four (or eight!). There are street musicians, storytellers, live animals, and many other things to entertain you along the way. Read all about them below.

AFRICAN ENTERTAINMENT

African music fills the air in the village of Harambe. Live bands perform here throughout the day.

ANIMAL ENCOUNTERS

Get to know our smaller animal friends as they roam through the park with their human keepers.

DINOLAND U.S.A. ENTERTAINMENT

A bunch of wacky performers is on the loose—and they will do anything to make you dig them! They usually drive around the area in a truck, stopping to make noise along the way.

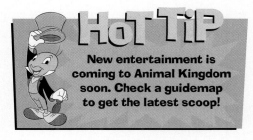

HoT TiP

New entertainment is coming to Animal Kingdom soon. Check a guidemap to get the latest scoop!

SAFARI VILLAGE ENTERTAINMENT

In this land storytellers tell animal tales, while music based on sounds of nature plays in the background.

Where to find CHARACTERS
at Disney's Animal Kingdom

It's easy to find Disney characters at Animal Kingdom—they have a land all their own. **Camp Minnie-Mickey** is the best place to meet characters in this park. Different characters hang out there all day. You might see Mickey, Goofy, Winnie the Pooh, Tigger, or other Disney favorites. Ask them to sign the autograph section at the end of this book.

Camp Minnie-Mickey isn't the only place to find characters in Animal Kingdom these days. They make appearances all over the theme park. So be on the lookout!

Donald Duck, Pluto, and other characters host breakfast at **Restaurantosaurus**.

Animal Kingdom TIPS

Animal Kingdom can get very hot, especially in the summer months. Head for Kali River Rapids or Conservation Station to cool off. And drink lots of water!

Go to the thrill rides—Dinosaur and Kali River Rapids—early, before they get too crowded, and don't forget to get a Fastpass.

On the Kilimanjaro Safaris ride, look at the back of the seat in front of you. The pictures will show you which animals you're about to see.

Check the Tip Board in Safari Village to find out how long the wait is for the most popular attractions.

It doesn't really matter what time you get to the safari—the animals are there all day long.

It's Tough to be a Bug! (inside The Tree of Life) is **very scary** to some kids. In it, bugs seem to shoot quills, spiders fall from above, and creepy critters scamper beneath your seat.

It's fun to see how many animals you can find carved into The Tree of Life and the other buildings in Safari Village.

Look for your favorite Disney characters in Camp Minnie-Mickey. It's the best place to find them in the park.

Can't find your parents? Ask the closest Disney cast member for help.

Check out the thunder and lightning effects inside the Rainforest Cafe.

Attraction Ratings

COOL
(Check It Out)

- The Oasis
- Flights of Wonder
- Cretaceous Trail
- Conservation Station

REALLY COOL
(Don't Miss)

- Tarzan Rocks!
- The Boneyard playground
- Maharajah Jungle Trek
- Pocahontas and Her Forest Friends

THE COOLEST
(See at Least Twice)

- Kilimanjaro Safaris
- Kali River Rapids
- Festival of the Lion King
- Dinosaur
- It's Tough to be a Bug!
- Pangani Forest Exploration Trail

Your favorite Animal Kingdom attractions

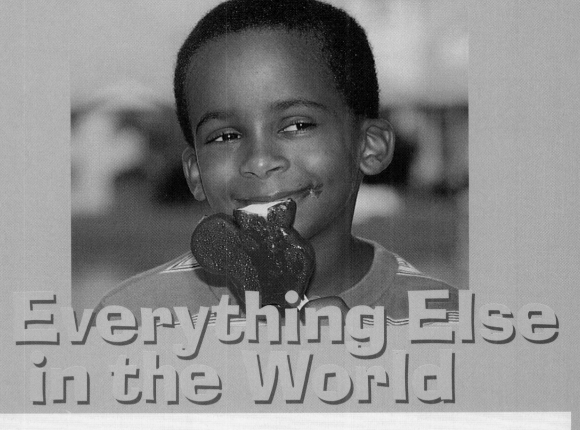

Everything Else in the World

No matter what you're interested in—water fun, sports, or animals—Walt Disney World has enough to make every minute of your vacation a blast. After you visit the theme parks, there's still so much to do. There are three water parks, speedy boats to rent, horses to ride, a gigantic arcade, and lots of neat shopping spots.

If you're into sports, check out Disney's Wide World of Sports complex, rent a bike, or try your hand at miniature golf. To test your detective skills, take one of Disney's special scavenger hunts.

In this chapter, you can read up on all the extra activities and find out about hotels and restaurants at Walt Disney World. Then you can help your family decide where to stay, where to eat, and what to do when you're not at the theme parks.

Party Puzzler

One of Disney's starlets is throwing a party and she has invited some of her most famous animated girlfriends. Each invited guest may take a date from her own movie. Use the date list to find out who is on the guest list. Write the names of the guests in the spaces below. When you're done, read the name that appears in the shaded area. She's throwing the party!

Guest List

Date List

1. Pongo
2. Woody
3. Prince Charming
4. Tarzan
5. Dopey
6. Lumière
7. Shang
8. Flik
9. Prince Eric
10. Aladdin

Waters of the World

It's easy to get wet, stay cool, and have fun at Walt Disney World. That's because it's a water wonderland. Choose from three water parks or take a dip in your hotel pool. If you're under the age of 10, you must bring a grown-up with you to the water parks.

Typhoon Lagoon

A typhoon is a powerful, windy storm. It dumps huge amounts of rain and sends objects flying through the air. This water park looks like a typhoon hit it. There's even a boat stuck on a mountain top! Of course, a storm didn't really put the boat there—Disney Imagineers did. They also put in pools, water slides, and a raft ride.

Catch a wave

The biggest pool here is like a small ocean. It has 5-foot waves. That makes body-surfing fun. There are also three speed slides to try. They send you zipping through a dark cave. For a calmer ride, you can slip into a tube and float along a river. Afterward, you can glide down more water slides.

There's also a special area just for younger kids—Ketchakiddee Creek. It has small slides and other games.

Swim with the sharks

Shark Reef is an amazing part of Typhoon Lagoon. It's the home of nurse sharks, bonnethead sharks, and leopard sharks. And you can splash around with them. Don't worry—these sharks are friendly. They don't mind when people swim in their tank. Are you brave enough to swim with the sharks? (You must be at least 10 years old.)

Blizzard Beach

Would you wear a bathing suit to a snow-covered mountain? Probably not. But you should wear one to Blizzard Beach. It looks like a place to ski, but it's really a water park. So don't worry if you can't ski. Nobody skis down the mountain here. They slide!

Reach the peak

Like a real ski resort, all the action centers around a mountain. In this case, it's Mount Gushmore. To get to the top, you can take a chair lift. The ride gives you a fantastic view of the whole park.

The scariest slide on the mountain is Summit Plummet. It begins 120 feet in the air, on a platform that looks like a ski jump. It drops you down a steep slide at about 60 miles per hour. That's faster than many cars go on the highway.

Slip-sliding away

There are plenty of other ways to slide down the mountain. Tube slides, body slides, and inner-tube rides can keep you busy all day long. It's fun to body-surf in the wave pool, too.

For preteens, there's Ski Patrol Training Camp, with its "iceberg" obstacle course, and ropes for swinging into the water. Tike's Peak is a special place for younger kids. It has slides and a snow-castle fountain play area.

As Karyn puts it, "This is one awesome water park."

READER TIP

"Go to a waterpark in the afternoon when it's hot and crowded at the theme parks. Then you can return to the theme park when it cools down in the evening."

Hailey (age 12)
Saranac, NY

River Country

This may be the smallest Disney water park, but you can still have big fun here. You can zip down water slides, shoot the rapids in a tube, and swing from a rope and then drop into the lake. *Kerplunk!*

Disney Imagineers got the idea for River Country from books by Mark Twain: *The Adventures of Tom Sawyer* and *The Adventures of Huckleberry Finn*. In both stories, the boys splash in their favorite swimming spot.

Tom and Huck don't visit River Country—but other characters sometimes do. Friends like Goofy, Chip, and Dale are here to celebrate the Fourth of July all summer long. You can meet them, play tug-of-war, and join in potato sack races during the All-American Water Party. You might even get picked to be in a special parade!

To find out when the party is happening, ask a parent to call 407-939-4636.

Let's Get Wet!

Many other places around Walt Disney World offer chances to get wet. At the Magic Kingdom, head for Splash Mountain and sit on the right side of the log. Or hang around Donald's Boat at Mickey's Toontown Fair. Ariel's Grotto also has squirting water to play in. At Epcot, go to the fountain between World Showcase and Future World. Or play in the mist at the Cool Wash outside of Test Track. At the Disney-MGM Studios, there is a fire hydrant on New York Street that squirts water. Nobody stays dry at Kali River Rapids in Disney's Animal Kingdom. There are squirting fountains at the Downtown Disney Marketplace, too.

Fort Wilderness

Fort Wilderness is tucked away in a wooded area of Walt Disney World. (It isn't really a fort. It's a campground.) You can stay overnight or just come for a day. There are tennis and volleyball courts, and a marina with lots of boats. River Country is also nearby. You could spend days here and not run out of things to do. If you only have a couple of hours, explore the petting farm and rent a boat for a ride around Bay Lake.

Everything Else in the World

Petting Farm

Chickens, goats, pigs, and sheep live on a small farm at Fort Wilderness. Some of the animals like people to pet them. Others enjoy eating pellets from kids' hands (you can buy their special food from a dispenser that looks like a gumball machine).

Most kids think the farm is fun. "You can get close to the animals without being afraid," says Lissy. Karyn says, "If you really like animals, you'll have fun no matter how old you are."

More Fort Wilderness Fun

Fort Wilderness offers lots of other things to do. You can rent a canoe for a trip along the campground's canals. Or you can rent a bicycle and explore one of the many trails. At the Tri-Circle-D Ranch, you can see the champion horses that pull the trolleys in the Magic Kingdom. (They live in a barn near Pioneer Hall.)

Kids over 9 years old can take a trail ride on horseback. You can also enjoy a Fort Wilderness hayride, go fishing, or rent a speedboat.

Sports

Kids who like sports can find plenty of ways to keep active at Walt Disney World.

You can rent boats or bikes at one of the resorts, or play miniature golf on one of Disney's themed courses. To see athletes at work, visit Disney's Wide World of Sports complex. Read on to find out how.

Water Mouse Boats

A Water Mouse is a speedy little boat that you can rent. And it delivers big thrills. If you are 12 or older, you can drive one all by yourself.

A Water Mouse ride gets very high marks from kids. "It's awesome," says Brian L. "I was turning into the waves and one splashed on top of me." David B. thinks it's neat to drive your own boat. "This is fun that you definitely can't miss," he says.

You can rent a Water Mouse boat at many Disney resorts. The cost is about $20 for a half hour.

Disney's Wide World of Sports Complex

Sports fans should plan a visit to this exciting complex. It has facilities for every sport you can imagine. The Atlanta Braves baseball team comes here for spring training. The Orlando Rays baseball team trains and plays here, too. (The O-Rays are a minor league team for the Tampa Bay Devil Rays.)

Watch a game

You can spend a day watching some amateur events. Tickets cost $7 for kids ages 3 through 9, and $9 for anyone 10 or older. If you want to see a professional game, you have to buy your tickets ahead of time. The prices vary. Have a parent call 407-363-6600 for information.

Play ball

Do you like to play football? If so, the NFL Experience activity area is perfect for you. There are places to practice running, passing, punting, and catching—just like the pros do! (It's on an outdoor field at the sports complex.)

Miniature Golf

Even if you've never held a golf club before, you'll do well at mini golf. It's fun to play, and full of surprises.

Fantasia Gardens

If you have seen the old movie *Fantasia*, you'll know how this miniature golf course got its name. Where else will you find hippos on tiptoe, dancing mushrooms, or xylophone stairs?

The holes are grouped by musical themes. At the Dance of the Hours hole, watch the hippo standing on an

alligator. If you hit the ball through the gator's mouth, the hippo dances!

The cost is $7.50 to play one round for kids ages 3 through 9, and $9.25 for anyone 10 or older.

Disney's Winter Summerland

Sometimes even Santa Claus needs a vacation. Just like you, he picked Walt Disney World as the perfect place to go and have fun.

As the story goes, Santa and his helpers built these mini-golf courses as a place to relax and enjoy the sun. That's why one looks like a beach, with sand castles and surfboards on it. But then the elves got homesick, so they built a second course that reminded them of the North Pole. Everything looks like it's covered in snow!

There are even igloos and jolly snowmen, and holes for ice fishing.

For a bit of a challenge, try the summer course. It's a little harder than the winter course. Santa is snoozing at one of the trickiest holes. You have to hit the ball across his lap without waking him up. The winter holes offer fun surprises, too. Get the ball in one of the holes and Mickey himself pops out of a present!

The cost is $7.50 to play on one course for kids ages 3 through 9, and $9.25 for anyone 10 or older.

Scavenger Hunts

If you are a fan of the tales told by Walt Disney World's shows and rides, you'll probably enjoy these special tours. Each one makes you feel like you are part of the story!

FAMILY MAGIC TOUR

This program is fun for the whole family. Parents and kids can join in a themed scavenger hunt through the Magic Kingdom. Guests search for the answers to different clues that lead to the missing item. If you go on this two-hour tour be sure to wear your sneakers—you'll be doing lots of walking! The cost is about $15 for kids 3 to 9, and $25 for everyone 10 and over. Parents should call 407-WDW-TOUR for reservations.

PIRATE CRUISE

Did you know that there is a pirate's treasure buried near the Magic Kingdom? It's said to be hidden somewhere in the Seven Seas lagoon. Each day an expedition just for kids sails out from the Grand Floridian in search of it. Do you think you are up to the challenge? The captain of the ship will give you a map and a series of puzzling clues to help you on your way. During the journey, kids get to snack on cold treats like ice cream and frozen juice bars. You have 1½ hours to find the treasure. And if you do, it's yours to keep! This program is for kids age 3 to 10. Cost is about $20 per child. Parents should call 407-WDW-DINE for reservations.

Who am I?

- I wear a flower for a crown
- I keep the workers in line
- I fell for a fellow named Flik

Answer: Atta

Downtown Disney

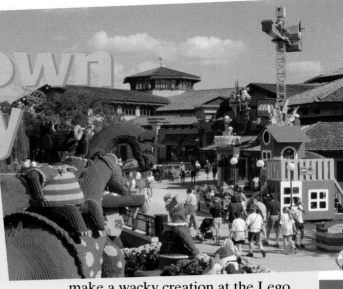

What has interesting shops and restaurants, movies, dance spots, boats to rent, and much more? Downtown Disney! It has three different sections: the West Side, the Marketplace, and Pleasure Island.

The West Side

This is the newest section of Downtown Disney. It has places to shop, eat, and catch a movie, plus DisneyQuest (read all about it on the next page).

There's even an exciting show by Cirque du Soleil (pronounced: *sirk due so-LAY*). It's performed in a building that looks like a giant circus tent—but this show's not like an ordinary circus! You won't see a Ring Master or wild animals. Instead, there are gymnasts and acrobats dressed in colorful costumes. They twist their bodies, and dance in unusual ways.

The Marketplace

Searching for that perfect souvenir? The best place to look is in the Marketplace. There are dozens of shops to browse in. You can also make a wacky creation at the Lego Imagination Center. As Kirsti says, "It's the coolest! You can build things. There are also life-size Lego models, like a painter, and a dinosaur. There's even a snoring man."

Amy's favorite place to shop is the World of Disney store. It's the biggest Disney store in the world.

Pleasure Island

You might think this place is just for grown-ups—but kids can have fun at Pleasure Island. Especially kids who like to dance. Kids can bring their parents to three clubs: the Wildhorse Saloon (country music), 8TRAX (1970s tunes), and Rock N Roll Beach Club (rock 'n' roll, of course).

If you don't dance, don't worry. There are also games to play, outdoor shows, and fireworks to watch every night. You can even get a temporary Mickey Mouse tattoo!

Hidden Mickey Alert!
Some of the Marketplace's dancing water fountains form the shape of you know who!

DisneyQuest

This place is probably bigger than any arcade you've ever seen! It's filled from top to bottom with every interactive game imaginable. With all the beeps and buzzers in this place, it sounds like you are standing in one giant video game. Even the elevator has special effects!

Pick a zone

DisneyQuest is separated into four different areas called "zones." In the **Explore Zone** you can visit far away places on virtual reality adventures. You might go on a pirate adventure or ride the rapids on a prehistoric jungle cruise.

The center of the **Score Zone** is a gigantic pinball game called Mighty Ducks Pinball Slam. In it, the people are giant joysticks! This zone is also the place to find all different kinds of brand-new games.

Future Imagineers will love the **Create Zone**. Here you can take a short animation class, try computer painting, or have stickers made out of your photo. You can also design your own roller coaster and then ride it on CyberSpace Mountain, a virtual reality ride that goes upside down and twists all around.

In the **Replay Zone** you get prizes for the points you earn on some of the games. Choose from favorites

READER TIP

"Expect a long line for CyberSpace Mountain at DisneyQuest. It's very popular!"

Veronica (age 11)
Bloomington, IN

like Skee Ball and Whack an Alien (it's the *Toy Story* version of Whack a Mole). There's also a room full of video games that were popular more than ten years ago. Ask your parents if they remember them.

Take a break

There is so much to choose from! The kids all agree that you could spend all day here. But it's also a good idea to take some breaks along the way. For a quick meal or a tasty dessert, stop by the Cheesecake Factory Express—it's inside DisneyQuest. "At some of the tables you can even surf the Internet while you eat," Eric says.

DisneyQuest costs about $22 for kids ages 3 through 9, and $28 for anyone 10 or older.

Walt Disney World Resorts

In all, there are 21 resorts on the Walt Disney World property. There are so many hotel rooms that you could stay in a different one every night for 55 years!

Just like the rides at the parks, each of the resorts has its own special theme. And all of the resorts are fun to stay at. But they are fun to visit, too. So if you have time, you might want to stop by some of them—to have a meal or just to enjoy the atmosphere.

Resorts near the
Magic Kingdom

CONTEMPORARY

This was the first Walt Disney World hotel. It looked very modern when it was built in 1971 (that's how it got its name). When it opened it had a talking elevator and a monorail station right in the middle of it. It still has these things today, plus a huge arcade and Chef Mickey's—one of the best character restaurants in Walt Disney World.

> **Contemporary Tip**
> In the center of the resort is a mural that's 90 feet tall. There are colorful pictures of children and animals all over it. One of the goats has 5 legs. See how long it takes you to spot him!

FORT WILDERNESS

Bring a camper or rent a cabin at this pretty wooded campground. This resort is full of activities. You can go for a hayride, visit the petting farm, or take a trip through the woods on a pony. At night, Chip and Dale come over to roast marshmallows by the campfire with the guests. This is also home to the popular dinner show called the Hoop-Dee-Doo Musical Revue.

> **Fort Wilderness Tip**
> There are lots of trees in the woods of Fort Wilderness. But there's only one that's famous. It's called the Lawn Mower Tree. You'll know why when you find it!

GRAND FLORIDIAN

This elegant hotel looks like a huge mansion from the 1900s. At first, it seems to be designed for grown-ups, but it's also fun for kids. There are special activities, like face painting and storytelling. At night you can sit in a big, comfy chair and listen to an old-fashioned band play in the main building. There is also a pretty pool with roses all around it. The monorail stops here, too.

Grand Floridian Tip

All the guests staying at this resort are given a special robe to use during their visit. If you're staying here, ask a parent to request a child-size robe for you!

The Monorail

The monorail connects the Magic Kingdom with the **Contemporary**, **Polynesian**, and **Grand Floridian** resorts. It's also the best way to get from the Magic Kingdom to Epcot or the Transportation and Ticket Center. At some stations a family can sit up front, with the driver. Ask a cast member if you can take a turn.

POLYNESIAN

The plants and trees at this hotel make it look like a tropical island. The live parrots and waterfalls in the main building make the setting seem real even when you're indoors. There's a pool that looks like it's part of a coral reef, and a beautiful beach with hammocks to rest on. The monorail also has a station here.

Polynesian Tip

Join the Big Kahuna in welcoming the night at the weekend torch-lighting ceremonies. Before the torches are lit, there is a terrific flame twirling act.

WILDERNESS LODGE

With its log columns and totem poles, this hotel looks like a national park from the American Northwest. The fireplaces and rocking chairs in the main building make you feel right at home. Outside there's an erupting geyser and a pool that looks like it's part of a hot spring. There are so many Hidden Mickeys here that there's even a tour and contest to see how many you can find!

Wilderness Lodge Tip

Look for the "Proterozoic Fossils and Minerals" display. It's a rock key to the strata of the giant Grand Canyon fireplace in the main lobby.

Resorts near
Epcot and the
Disney-MGM Studios

BOARDWALK

This hotel is designed to look like Atlantic City, New Jersey, once did. Just like on an old-fashioned boardwalk, there are games and snack stands here for everyone to enjoy. You can rent a special bicycle built for four, or swim in a pool that looks like an amusement park.

BoardWalk Tip
Look for a crystal globe under a chandelier in the main building. It's actually a Disney time capsule that will be opened on Walt Disney World's 50th anniversary.

READER TIP
"Try the entertainment offered by many of the hotels, like fishing or boating. It's great fun!"
Amber (age 14)
Jenison, MI

DIXIE LANDINGS

The buildings at this hotel look like mansions and country homes from the Old South. The food court is designed after a cotton mill and it has a real working waterwheel that's 30 feet tall. Inside you can actually see the cotton being pressed.

Dixie Landings Tip
If you like to fish, head down to the Ol' Fishin' Hole. The resort has poles to rent and worms to buy.

CARIBBEAN BEACH

This happy and colorful hotel looks like the islands of the Caribbean. You can have fun in the sun all day at its beaches and pools.

Caribbean Beach Tip
Don't worry about packing a sand bucket or shovel—the kids meals at the food court come with them!

OLD KEY WEST

The townhouses that make up this resort have all the comforts of home. The palm trees and sunny design make it a very warm and welcoming place.

Old Key West Tip
Kids ages 5 through 10 can sign up for an Un-Birthday Party. You'll enjoy the games and the cupcake that comes with it.

145

THE VILLAS AT THE DISNEY INSTITUTE

There are several types of villas, including the "treehouses" on thick stilts. Some villas are set in the woods, while others are by the beach. There are lots of outdoor activities to do here and a big spa for taking a relaxing break.

The Villas at the Disney Institute Tip

Hop on a bicycle and explore the resort's shaded backroads, or rent a canoe and paddle around the Disney Institute canals.

PORT ORLEANS

The special details at this hotel make it look like the city it's named for—New Orleans, Louisiana. There's a long river, and a fun pool with a curving dragon slide.

Port Orleans Tip

The best way to get from this resort to Downtown Disney is on a boat—it's called the Sassagoula River Cruise. It also takes you to Dixie Landings, where guests staying at Port Orleans can use the pools and playground.

YACHT AND BEACH CLUB

These two connected hotels are designed after the homes near the beaches of Massachusetts. Even the pool makes you feel like you're at the beach—the bottom of it is covered with real sand!

Yacht and Beach Club Tip

Be sure to bring your sneakers. One of the best parts about staying here is that you can walk from the hotel to Epcot or the BoardWalk.

SWAN AND DOLPHIN

You can't miss the dolphin and swan statues that sit on top of these two hotels—they're gigantic. Together the hotels have lots to do and many restaurants to eat at. (One is a fun ice cream parlor called Dolphin Fountain.) You can walk to Epcot from both hotels.

Swan and Dolphin Tip

There are 250 swan and dolphin statues at this resort. Some are big, but some are very small. See how many you can spot.

READER TIP

"If you stay at a Disney hotel, make sure to ask for a wake-up call. It's usually Mickey or one of his friends."

Raquel (age 7)
Miami, FL

Resorts near
Animal Kingdom

READER TIP

"If you get a chance, you should go swimming at your hotel's pool at night. It's lots of fun!"

Laura (age 11)
Alexandria, VA

ALL-STAR RESORTS

There are three All-Star resorts, and each of them has its own theme— sports, music, or movies. It's easy to tell which All-Star you're at, because they have giant icons that are even bigger than the buildings. At All-Star Music look for the big cowboy boots. A huge football helmet shows you you're at All-Star Sports. And when you see a 38-foot-tall Buzz Lightyear, there's no doubt you're at the All-Star Movies.

All-Star Tip

There are many Hidden Mickeys to hunt for. Start your search at the main statues in each of the resorts.

CORONADO SPRINGS

The land at this hotel looks like parts of the Southwestern U.S. and Mexico. The buildings are the color of clay. There's a pool that looks like an ancient pyramid with a slide that passes under a spitting jaguar. Beside it is a sandbox with ancient treasures waiting to be uncovered.

Coronado Springs Tip

Some of the food at the restaurant here might be new to you. If you don't like Mexican food, be sure to order from the kid's menu.

Disney Cruise Line

Set sail on a Disney ship with Mickey and his friends. You visit Walt Disney World for a few days and then cruise to the Caribbean. There you can explore Disney's private island, Castaway Cay. Each ship has special activity areas, pools, and programs just for kids, so you can do your own thing while your parents relax.

ANIMAL KINGDOM LODGE

Creatures like giraffes, zebras, gazelles, and beautiful birds live near this new hotel. The trees and animals make it seem like the resort is set in a real African savanna. A giant mud fireplace and thatched ceilings add to the feeling that you are at a big campsite in Africa.

Animal Kingdom Lodge Tip

Almost all of the rooms have excellent views of the animals. But if you want an even closer look, remember to bring a pair of binoculars from home.

Everything Else in the World

147

Restaurants

Eating at Walt Disney World can be as much fun as riding Splash Mountain (well, almost as much fun!). Here are our suggestions for the best spots in each theme park to head to for your favorite foods.

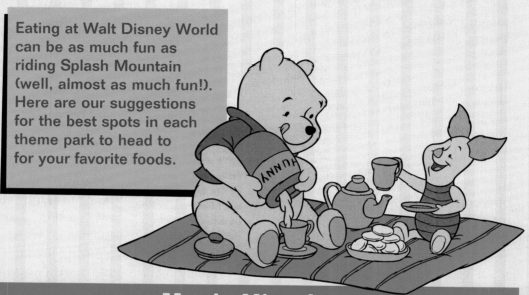

Magic Kingdom
Best Places for Favorite Foods

Candy and rice crispie treats . . . . Main Street Confectionery
Chicken fingers . . . . Crystal Palace
Chili . . . . Pecos Bill Cafe
Chocolate chip cookies . . . . Main Street Bake Shop
Cinnamon pretzels . . . . Fantasyland Pretzel Stand
Fruit . . . . Liberty Square Market
Hamburgers . . . . Pinocchio Village Haus
Hot dogs . . . . Casey's Corner
Ice cream . . . . Plaza Ice Cream Parlor
Macaroni and cheese . . . . Cinderella's Royal Table
Peanut butter and jelly sandwiches . . . . Aunt Polly's Dockside Inn
Pizza . . . . Plaza Pavilion
Turkey legs . . . . Lunching Pad at Rockettower Plaza
Veggie burgers . . . . Cosmic Ray's Starlight Cafe

Epcot
Best Places for Favorite Foods

Cookies . . . . Kringla Bakeri og Kafe (in Norway)

Egg rolls . . . . Lotus Blossom Cafe (in China)

Fried dough . . . . Trapper Bob's Beaver Tail Cart (in Canada)

Fruit . . . . Pure and Simple (in Wonders of Life)

Gummy Bears . . . . Süssigkeiten (in Germany)

Hamburgers . . . . Liberty Inn (in The American Adventure)

Hot dogs . . . . Electric Umbrella (in Innoventions)

Ice cream . . . . Refreshment Port (near Canada)

Macaroni and cheese . . . . Pasta and Potato Stand (in The Land)

Nachos . . . . Cantina de San Angel (in Mexico)

Peanut butter and jelly sandwiches . . . . . . Sandwich Shop (in The Land)

Soft pretzels . . . . Sommerfest (in Germany)

Spaghetti . . . . Alfredo's (in Italy)

Disney-MGM Studios
Best Places for Favorite Foods

Caramel apples . . . . Sweet Spells
Cookies . . . . The Writer's Stop
Fruit . . . . Anaheim Produce (in the Sunset Ranch Market)
Hamburgers . . . . ABC Commissary
Hot dogs . . . . . . Rosie's All-American Cafe (in the Sunset Ranch Market)
Ice cream . . . . Dinosaur Gertie's Ice Cream of Extinction
Macaroni and cheese . . . . Hollywood & Vine
Peanut butter and jelly sandwiches . . . . 50's Prime Time Cafe
Pizza . . . . .Toy Story Pizza Planet
Spaghetti . . . . Mama Melrose's Ristorante Italiano
Turkey legs . . . . Catalina Eddie's (in the Sunset Ranch Market)
Veggie burgers . . . . Sci-Fi Dine-In Theater

Animal Kingdom
Best Places for Favorite Foods

Candy . . . . Island Mercantile
Chicken nuggets and fries . . . . Restaurantosaurus
Chocolate-covered marshmallows . . . . Sweet Cart
Cookies . . . . Chip 'n' Dale's Cookie Cabin
Fried chicken. . . . . Tusker House
Fruit . . . . Harambe Fruit Market
Hamburgers. . . . . Mr. Kamal's Burger Grill
Hot dogs . . . . Munch Wagon
Ice cream and frozen yogurt . . . . Tamu Tamu Refreshments
Pizza . . . . Pizzafari
Turkey legs . . . . Dino Diner
Veggie burgers . . . . Rainforest Cafe

Snack Wagons

All around the theme parks are wagons that sell soft drinks and quick snacks. The ice cream, popcorn, pretzels, and fruit really hit the spot!

Eating with the Characters

Kids of all ages enjoy eating with the characters. It's one of the best ways to see your favorite Disney stars. They will come right up to your table to meet you. Bring a camera because the characters are also happy to pose for photos. And don't forget your pen so you can collect some autographs!

Each of the theme parks has at least one restaurant that invites the characters over. Many of the resorts have character meals, too. They are very popular, so no matter which restaurant your family chooses, it's a good idea to make priority seating arrangements ahead of time. Ask a parent to call 407-WDW-DINE (939-3463).

Character meals aren't just fun because you get to see the characters. They're special because the food is served in a special way. Depending on which restaurant you choose, the meal will either be presented in a buffet or family-style. Picky eaters may prefer one of the buffets—with so much to choose from, you're sure to find something you like!

Dinner Shows

Hoop-Dee-Doo Musical Revue

Entertainers sing, dance, and tell jokes while you chow down on chicken, ribs, and corn. Danielle G. says, "They get everyone in on the fun and put on a wonderful show." David B. thinks it's "very funny. I was laughing the whole time," he says.

Mickey's Backyard Barbecue

Mickey's having a barbecue, and you are welcome to join the fun. You can eat all the hot dogs, barbecued ribs, and strawberry shortcake you want, while a live band plays country music. After dinner, there's a show for kids, games, and dancing with the Disney characters.

Polynesian Luau

Aloha! That means "hello" (and "goodbye") in Hawaiian. You'll hear it a lot at this show. Performers do the hula and other Hawaiian dances, while waiters serve Polynesian food and fruity punch.

Wonderland Tea Party

It's tea time at 1900 Park Fare in the Grand Floridian resort. Some afternoons Characters from *Alice in Wonderland* throw a lunch party just for kids. You can decorate cupcakes, sip tea, listen to a story, and play party games.

Reservations for all of these shows should be made before you arrive at Walt Disney World. Your parents can call 407-WDW-DINE (939-3463).

Magical Memories

The fun doesn't have to end when your vacation does. Use these pages to preserve your Disney memories.

These are the people I vacationed with:

I arrived at Walt Disney World on:
_____
(month/day/year)
I stayed for _____ days.

My first day at Walt Disney World I went to:

I traveled to Walt Disney World by:
[ ] car
[ ] plane
[ ] bus
[ ] boat
[ ] train

The name of our hotel was:

I went on this ride first:

My usual bedtime is _____ o'clock.

During my trip, the latest I went to bed was _____ o'clock.

The earliest I woke up was _____ o'clock.

Draw your favorite
Disney character here!

The weather at
Walt Disney World was:

[ ] sunny
[ ] rainy
[ ] windy
[ ] chilly
[ ] snowy

This attraction
wasn't what
I expected:

It surprised me
because it was:

The scariest ride I went on was:

My favorite ride was:

I went on it_____times.

Tape a used
Walt Disney World
ticket here!

If I were an Imagineer,
this is the ride
I would design:

My least favorite
ride was:

I didn't like it
because it was:

Magical Memories

The best Disney theme park was:

[ ] **Magic Kingdom**
[ ] **Epcot**
[ ] **Disney-MGM Studios**
[ ] **Disney's Animal Kingdom**

Vacations aren't just fun, they're educational, too! One thing that I learned at Walt Disney World is:

My favorite restaurant was:

I ate:

Building a theme park was Walt Disney's dream. What's your dream?

The funniest thing that happened at Walt Disney World was:

Paste a Walt Disney World vacation photo here!